50
plus one

Greatest Cities in the World You Should Visit

by
Paul J. Christopher

Information to Encourage Achievement

1261 West Glenlake
Chicago, IL 60660
www.encouragementpress.com

ISBN: 1-933766-01-8
EAN: 978-1-933766-01-0

10 9 8 7 6 5 4 3 2 1
♻ printed on recycled paper

©2007 Encouragement Press, LLC
1261 West Glenlake
Chicago, IL 60660

Greatest Cities in the World You Should Visit

Acknowledgements

Special thanks…and cheers to the following:

Jennifer Fester, Heather Hutchins, Greg Lackner and Martin Stich

Table of Contents

Introduction

Imagine holding the whole world in your hands—or at least the greatest cities of the world! That is exactly what this book is about: The excitement and allure of the exotic, beautiful, legendary and famous cities of the world. Each is a center of art, culture, architecture, business and cuisine. Each has its own unique appeal, its own charm, and its own fascinating and fact-filled history.

Part travel book, part travelogue and part wish book, *50 plus one Greatest Cities of the World You Should Visit* is an intimate, easy and satisfying visit to the world's most wonderful cities. Imagine how helpful a book like this will be when planning that trip of a lifetime. With just a quick read, you can narrow down your travel choices to those most attractive to you.

Fascinated by history, geography, travel and culture? This is the perfect book for those interested in knowledge for its own sake. *50 plus one Greatest Cities of the World You Should Visit* provides information on everything from geography and climate to the history and sites you must see when you travel.

Love trivia? Sure, everyone does! Each chapter contains little-known facts and figures, unique to the city, its people and its culture.

While all the cities are presented in alphabetical order—there were too many disagreements to rank them otherwise—one city is our 50 *plus one* favorite: Paris! As many world travelers know well, Paris is the most popular and important travel destination in the world. Paris is alive with culture, art, history and cuisine. What is more, the city's compactness makes for easy and pleasant exploration. Paris is a walker's dream come true.

Enjoy your visits to Paris and the other greatest cities of the world. Happy reading and happy traveling!

Paul J. Christopher

plus one

Paris, France

The Basic Facts

Paris is the capital of France and is its largest city. Many consider Paris one of the most beautiful cities in the world, and it has been nicknamed the City of Light. During the late 20th century, Paris underwent a major facelift: modern structures replaced unusable buildings, but historically and aesthetically valuable buildings were restored and preserved. Some Parisians believe that the construction of skyscrapers has ruined the overall beauty of the city. Paris, however, continues to be a treasure trove of art, music, architecture and great food, and is one of the most visited cities in the world.

Geography

Paris lies at 48 degrees 51 minutes north latitude and 2 degrees 20 minutes east longitude. The city is located in the heart of a lowland called the Paris basin, some 100 miles southeast of the English Channel. The Seine River, an enduring symbol of the city, winds its way roughly eight miles through Paris from east to west. The Right Bank (La Rive Droite) and the Left Bank (La Rive Gauche) are located north and south of the river, respectively.

The layout of the city has evolved over hundreds of years. The Ile de la Cité, an island in the Seine, is the site on which Paris was founded and is considered the heart of the city. Paris contains many broad avenues, of which the most famous is the Champs-Élysées.

Climate

The Paris climate is moderate throughout the year and rarely reaches extremes of either cold or warmth. Winter temperatures average in the mid-40s Fahrenheit and summer temperatures average in the mid-70s Fahrenheit. Spring is considered the most beautiful time of year in Paris.

Government

Paris is divided into 20 arondissements, administrative divisions that are governed by independent commissions and mayors. Paris also has a central government that handles overall municipal services and laws; a mayor and 109 city council members are elected for 6-year terms.

Demographics

Paris is one of the most densely populated cities in the world. Gentrification and congestion have contributed to a rise in the cost of housing. As a result, the population of the city proper has decreased over the years, and many city residents have relocated to the nearby suburbs. Paris is a multicultural city; nearly 20 percent of its current population originated elsewhere in France or in other countries. Most city residents are of European background, but recent immigrants have come mainly from China, Africa and the Middle East. Paris currently has about 2.1 million residents.

Economy

Paris and the surrounding area comprise France's major industrial center. Products manufactured here include automobiles, chemicals, dyes and electronic equipment. Paris is also a center for printing and publishing. Smaller manufacturers in the city create Paris' world-renowned jewelry, perfume and haute couture women's clothing.

Paris is France's center of financial, marketing and distribution services. Tourism accounts for much of the city's economy and attracts thousands of visitors every year who seek the city's rich mixture of art, culture, architecture, music and food.

The History

The first residents of the area (on the Ile de la Cité around 250 B.C.) were a Celtic tribe named the Parisii. Roman invaders established a colony in the area in 52 B.C. The colony expanded quickly on both banks of the Seine and the settlement became known as Paris around 300 A.D. Paris was first made the capital of France in 512 by Clovis, the first ruler of the Frankish kingdom. As France and its rulers grew in power, so did Paris, and by the early 13th century the city was already recognized as a center of culture, education and government.

During the Renaissance, new boulevards, palaces and squares were styled to reflect ancient Greek and Roman architecture. The French monarchy held total control of France until the bloody French Revolution of 1789-1799, during which Paris served as the focal point. After a period of instability following the revolution, Napoléon Bonaparte (later Napoléon III, emperor from 1852-1870) took control of the government and made further improvements to the city, including banks, hospitals, theaters and infrastructure.

Long-range German cannons damaged Paris during World War I, but the city survived. In World War II, however, the German army occupied Paris during the years 1939-1945. Nevertheless, Paris became a center of the French underground (known as La Résistance). In 1944 Allied troops freed the city, which remained largely undamaged by the occupation.

The Sights and Sounds

Paris is undoubtedly the *plus one* city of the world. Visitors are overwhelmed by the city's richness, sophistication and artistry, and each neighborhood has its own characteristic sights and sounds. Paris' city center is compact and its transit system is first-rate, making it a wonderful city for visitors to explore.

One of the standouts in Paris is certainly Notre Dame de Paris, the famous cathedral that stands on the eastern half of the Île de la Cité. For nearly 2,000 years, Parisians have worshipped on this site. The present cathedral is actually the fourth church built on the site. Construction began in 1163, and the cathedral was not completed until the mid-14th century–nearly 300 years later! Take the 422-step hike to the top of the Bell Tower for a wonderful view of Paris and the cathedral itself. Notre Dame was heavily damaged during the French Revolution by mobs who viewed it as a symbol of the hated monarchy. Restorations in the mid-1800s added modern touches to the cathedral. It is known for its flying buttresses, which strengthen the walls while enabling natural light to shine through rose windows of beautiful stained glass.

Paris' two island quarters, Ile de la Cité and Ile St-Louis, are located in the Seine River. These areas delight locals and visitors alike, and they embody the beauty and wonder of traditional Paris: great sights, tree-lined streets, historic houses, and leisurely cafes and restaurants.

While Notre Dame de Paris is known throughout the world, many visitors rave about the Holy Chapel, La Sainte-Chapelle. This chapel was built in the years 1246-1248 for Louis IX, who became its patron. Its stained glass–perhaps the oldest in Paris–constitutes most of the upper chapel's walls. To construct the chapel in this way must have been a remarkable feat for its time!

New York has Fifth Avenue, Chicago has Michigan Avenue, but Paris has the Champs-Élysées: the world's greatest and most chic (read: expensive) shopping and restaurant center. This avenue, a little over a mile long, is not what it used to be; fast-food restaurants and car dealerships now encroach on this historic area.

Still, visitors flock to this avenue, often beginning their tour of Paris at the Arc de Triomphe. The Tuileries Gardens offers a beautiful end to a tour of this district. This 63-acre formal garden, which has often been painted by Paris' greatest artists, is so majestic that visitors enjoy lingering in its environs.

Perhaps Napoléon's finest contribution to Paris is the Arc de Triomphe, which towers more than 165 feet over the Champs-Élysées. It was commissioned to celebrate Napoléon's great military successes; ironically, construction was completed many years after his death. The Tomb of the Unknown Soldier is located under the Arc, and memorializes the French who perished in the First and Second World Wars. French victories and other special events are typically celebrated here.

Napoléon is buried in Mansart's Dome at Les Invalides, founded in 1674 as a home for older, ailing soldiers. Fittingly, the army museum is near by and famous of its collection of arms and armaments.

What can be said about a royal palace that is today the world's greatest art museum? The Louvre has everything to satisfy the artistic eye. There is simply no end to the degree and depth of this museum's collection. Exhibits include the 140-carat Regent Diamond, the Venus de Milo, and Leonardo da Vinci's renowned Mona Lisa. The Louvre's Egyptian collection is world famous, but its Greek, European, French and Arab collections are just as impressive.

The Place de la Concorde is a large–and congested–quarter of Paris worthy of attention. In this square, neoclassical buildings surround a 75-foot-tall, 3,000-year old Egyptian obelisk and its two nearby fountains. The annual Tour de France bicycle race ends here, as do most parades.

Care for a bird's eye view from 1,000 feet? Take the elevator to the Eiffel Tower, which was built for the World Exhibition of 1889. Although most French considered the tower to be an eyesore, it now stands as the most recognizable symbol of this great city.

The Pompidou Center is a museum with a decidedly futuristic appearance: the building's steel beams and its heating, water, and electric systems are located on the exterior. The museum's main attraction, naturally, is the National Museum of Modern Art, encompassing most every conceivable style and school of 20th century art.

The Orsay Museum, while not exclusively French in character, contains an expansive collection of Impressionist art. In many ways, this museum's collection complements that of the Louvre.

Paris, like many of the world's greatest cities, is on the go 24 hours a day. The cafes, clubs, sights and sounds are exhilarating and at times exhausting for visitors. The French and particularly the Parisians consider their city home to the greatest cuisine and chefs in the world. Why argue? Splurge a little and enjoy the other side of Paris: its food, wine, beer and coffee. Stay out after dark and take a boat ride along the Seine.

The Trivia

Fact: The Louvre, constructed in the 12th century and arguably the most famous art museum in the world, began as a fortress. The building was razed and rebuilt as a royal palace in the 1500s; additions over the years made it the largest palace in the world. In 1793 parts of the palace became a public museum, which displayed artwork formerly held by the deposed French royalty.

Fact: In 1914, during World War I, the Germans came within 15 miles of Paris. The French army used taxicabs to transport fresh soldiers to the front. This taxicab army helped the French defeat the Germans in the First Battle of the Marne, thereby averting a quick German victory.

Fact: Paris is laid out according to plans that evolved over the centuries. The Ile de la Cité is in the heart of the city. The Seine River runs from east to west through the city and divides it into the Right Bank and the Left Bank. The Right Bank contains the city's offices, small factories and some shops. The Left Bank has traditionally been a center for artists and students.

Fact: Victor Hugo's famous character, Quasimodo, found sanctuary in the cathedral of Notre Dame de Paris; this fictional character is almost as famous as the church itself.

Fact: To save Paris from destruction by the Nazis in World War II, the French government declared it an open city, which meant that the French did not defend it. German troops entered the city without opposition and marched down the Champs Elysees in triumph.

Fact: During the height of the French Revolution, executions were carried out on the Place de la Concorde. It is estimated that more than 1,000 people, including King Louis XVI and Queen Marie Antoinette were guillotined on this site.

Why Paris Is First Among World Cities

Paris was chosen as the first among the world's greatest cities because it has everything a city should have: nightlife, culture, art, architecture, history, fine cuisine and sophistication. Throughout history, the city was caught in the middle of political and social change and intrigue, yet the city and its treasures have survived and thrived to this day. Governments come and go, but Paris lives on. It is the symbol of style, haute culture, luxury and fine living. Who can visit Paris and not want to return?

1

Alexandria, Egypt

The Basic Facts

Alexandria is the second largest city in Egypt and the country's largest port. The city is often called the Pearl of the Mediterranean, as its culture and atmosphere tend more toward pan-Mediterranean than Middle Eastern.

Geography

Alexandria lies 31 degrees 12 minutes north latitude and 29 degrees 58 minutes east longitude. The city is located on the Mediterranean Sea in northwest Egypt, about 140 miles from Cairo. It is a mile from Lake Mariout and near the outlets of the Salam Canal and Rosetta River, which emanate from the Nile. Alexandria is built on the former island of Pharos, which was eventually connected to the mainland.

Climate

Alexandria has a relatively moderate climate for Northern Africa. Annual precipitation amounts to a mere eight inches, most of which falls during the months of December and January. Annual temperatures range from the mid-50s Fahrenheit in winter to the low 80s Fahrenheit in summer. This mild weather enables tourists to wander comfortably throughout the city.

Demographics

The vast majority of Alexandria's population was born in Egypt, although there are small concentrations of Bedouins, as well as Palestinian and Sudanese refugees. Islam is the majority religion, constituting nearly 90 percent of the inhabitants; the remaining residents are primarily adherents of Coptic Orthodox Christianity. Alexandria is estimated to have between 3.5 million and five million residents.

Economy

Alexandria's strategic location along the southern Mediterranean Coast has made it an important industrial center and port in Egypt. Major natural gas and oil pipelines originate in the nearby Suez Canal. Nearly 80 percent of Egypt's imports and exports flow through the city's harbors. Tourism is a vital facet of the economy as well. International tourists visit to explore Alexandria's rich historical past, as well as to escape nearby Cairo when the summer heat becomes unbearable.

The History

The city is named for Alexander the Great, who founded the city in 323 B.C. after conquering ancient Egypt. Under Ptolemy, Alexandria later became the capital of Egypt. The city had already become a major trade center, and its population grew rapidly. After Rome conquered Egypt in 30 B.C., the Roman Empire took full advantage of Alexandria's port to expand its reach in the Mediterranean. Over the next 2 millennia, various entities controlled the city: the Arabs, who moved the national capital to Cairo; the Ottomans; the Napoleonic French; and finally the British, who employed Alexandria as a naval base in both World Wars. The British withdrew from Egypt in the early 1950s and the country became a sovereign nation.

The Sights and Sounds

Unfortunately, little of the ancient city of Alexandria survives today. Prominent buildings were destroyed either by natural forces or were razed for reconstruction. Among the few monuments that remain to this day is Pompey's Pillar, located in the acropolis next to the Arab cemetery. The pillar is a 99-foot edifice of red granite that was once part of a temple colonnade.

Kom al Sukkfa, the catacombs of Alexandria, are a short distance from Pompey's Pillar. This labyrinth of graves and chambers is on several levels and contains ancient pillars, statues and sarcophagi accentuated with Egyptian and Roman inscriptions. Kom al Dikka is a contemporary excavation in the city proper; to date archaeologists have discovered the ruins of an ancient theatre and Roman baths.

The oldest section of Alexandria lies along the causeway that links the former island of Pharos to the mainland. The city districts that comprise the Turkish Quarter are Gumrok, Anfushi, and Ras el-Tin. The Quarter forms a T-shape that divides Alexandria's eastern and western harbors. The Bibliotheca Alexandrina attempts to recreate the Library of Alexandria, famous throughout the world as the storehouse of countless ancient papyrus scrolls. The contemporary granite-and-glass structure is a fascinating complex of museums, galleries, and research laboratories, and also has a planetarium and large reading room.

Alexandria's Greek Quarter is one of the finest residential districts in the city. Wealthy Greeks lived here at the turn of the century and the street names still reflect its Greek heritage. Notable landmarks here include the church of St. Saba and the Shallalat Gardens, on the site of the former Bab Rosetta fortification. The Zoological Gardens, the Museum of Natural History, and the Fine Arts Museum are located in close proximity, and public gardens extend into the surrounding area of the Antoniadis Palace.

Among the famous Islamic sites in the city are the Attarine Mosque, once a Christian church; Fort Qaitbey, built in the 1480s on the site of the ancient lighthouse at Pharos; the Mosque of Abu al-Abbas al-Mursi, Alexandria's largest and most important shrine; the Mostafa Kamel Graveyard, with four tombs that date to the 2nd century B.C.; the Muntazah Complex, a 115 acres palace with magnificent gardens; Shatby Tomb, the oldest of its kind in the city; and Terbana Mosque, one of the few remaining ancient mosques in Alexandria.

The Trivia

Fact: Another famous Muhammad Ali—no apparent relation to the world-famous boxing champion—was an Ottoman army officer who ruled Egypt after the French were ousted from the country. Ali helped to revive Alexandria's regional importance, which had waned for centuries as the city languished as a fishing village.

Fact: The Lighthouse of Alexandria is considered one of the Seven Wonders of the Ancient World, and the only one with a practical usage. This lighthouse ensured sailors a safe return to the harbor. It was the tallest building in the world at the time; with its foundation, the lighthouse stood nearly 400 feet. Its mirror reflected the sun's rays during the day, and could be seen more than 35 miles offshore. A large fire was the source of nighttime light for the structure; fuel for the fire was lifted through the tower's internal core. The building's summit was adored with a statue of Poseidon, the Greek god of the sea.

Fact: The Library at Alexandria once boasted a collection of half a million delicate papyrus scrolls, its contents detailing the vast body of knowledge discovered by the scientists and historians of the ancient world. Papyrus was invented by the Egyptians and was a primary export during that era.

Why Alexandria Is a *50 plus one* City

So many civilizations have left their mark on this fascinating city. Although much of its history is lost to the ages, what remains offers tourists a glimpse into the importance of this Mediterranean city. Today the city thrives as a vibrant center for regional and international trade. Alexandria is a great city because it is cosmopolitan, known for its rich culture as well as for its historical prominence.

2

Amsterdam, The Netherlands

The Basic Facts

Amsterdam is the capital of the Netherlands and the country's largest city. Second only to Rotterdam as the Netherlands' busiest port, Amsterdam is undoubtedly the cultural and financial center of the nation. Its name is derived from the Amstel River which flows through its confines.

Geography

Amsterdam lies at 52 degrees 21 minutes north latitude and 4 degrees 52 minutes east longitude. The city is located in North Holland Province on the banks of the IJsselmeer near The Hague. Amsterdam is a flat city, most of which is below sea level. The metropolis rests on a foundation of piles driven through peat and sand to the underlying clay substratum. The city's many canals are famous the world over and are a popular attraction for visitors. Amsterdam is linked to the North Sea and to other European countries by a network of railways, highways and canals. Amsterdam Schiphol Airport is one of Europe's busiest and continues to expand with increasing traffic to and from the Netherlands.

Climate

Amsterdam has a temperate climate similar to that of England; winters are mild and summers are rarely uncomfortably hot. Annual temperatures range from the mid-30s Fahrenheit in winter to the mid-50s Fahrenheit in summer. The city receives a considerable amount of rain throughout the year—a boon to the area's well-known symbol, the tulip, its blooms becoming a colorful carpet each spring.

Government

Amsterdam's government consists of a mayor, aldermen, and a municipal council. During the 1980s, as a means to improve municipal services, Amsterdam was divided into 15 boroughs. Local decisions are made at the borough level, but matters that concern the entire city, such as infrastructure improvements, are decided by the municipal council. Although Amsterdam is the official capital of the country, the seat of government is located in The Hague.

Demographics

The population of Amsterdam numbers approximately 735,000 and the metropolitan area's population is roughly 1.3 million. More than 170 nationalities are represented among the citizens, making Amsterdam one of the world's most culturally-diverse cities. Roman Catholicism is the dominant religion; minority groups include Protestant Christians and Muslims. Nearly 86 percent of the population is under the age of 65.

Economy

Amsterdam's strategic location in the European Union (EU) makes the city an important commercial center. The European headquarters of many international corporations are located here. Amsterdam's leading industries are shipbuilding, sugar refining, publishing, beer brewing, and manufacturing. Goods produced here include heavy machinery, paper products, textiles and clothing, porcelain, glass, aircraft parts, automobiles, and chemicals. Amsterdam is also recognized worldwide as a center for diamond cutting and polishing. The service industry is a major employer as well, and includes banking, insurance, and tourism.

The History

Amsterdam was founded in the 13th century and joined the Hanseatic League in 1369. By the middle of the 16th century, the city was swept up in the Protestant Reformation. Religious tolerance attracted Flemish merchants, Jewish diamond cutters, and French Huguenots, thus enhancing the size and diversity of the city's population. Amsterdam quickly became a burgeoning trade center, as merchants moved their goods through its ports to the rest of the Netherlands and to Western Europe.

Amsterdam became the capital of the Kingdom of the Netherlands. Even today, royals are typically crowned in Amsterdam, although they reside in a palace outside the city. The Nazi occupation during World War II devastated the city, and the government—which by then had been taken over by the Nazis—nearly wiped out the city's considerable Jewish population. Amsterdam slowly but steadily recovered from the destruction of the war to once again become a great European city.

The Sights and Sounds

Amsterdam, being a compact and flat city, is a walker's dream. The streets of the old city radiate outward from the many canals. Veteran tourists often suggest beginning at Central Station, which was built in 1903 and remains an important hub for intercity rail transportation.

The Beurs van Berlage is the home of the former Amsterdam Stock Exchange and is considered an architectural masterpiece. The building was designed by the architect Hendrick Petrus Berlage and constructed of red brick. The Weighthouse, which dates from 1616, was originally used to weigh the large quantities of hennep (cannabis) that passed through the city's ports. This building is located in an area called New Market, the oldest part of the city.

Amsterdam is famous as the hiding place of the diarist Anne Frank, her family and friends. The young author hid for 2 years in an attic in her father's office building, desperate to avoid discovery by the Nazis. The group was later betrayed and captured, and in 1945 Anne Frank died of typhus in 1945 while interned in a concentration camp. Her father Otto published her writings in 1947. *The Diary of a Young Girl*, as it is known in English, is a much-beloved autobiography that details her struggle to survive amid the Nazi occupation of Amsterdam. The book became an international sensation and was adapted for stage and screen. The building where she lived for those 2 years is now the Anne Frank Museum, and is dedicated to her memory and to the eradication of persecution and discrimination.

The Netherlands Maritime Museum has an extensive collection of restored sailing ships and vessel. The Weepers' Tower is a 15th century lookout, where women scanned the seas for their seafaring husbands, in hopes of a safe return from their long voyages abroad. The Golden Bend on the Gentleman's Canal is known for its beautiful 17th century homes where the wealthy merchant class moved in their search for upward mobility.

The Dutch artist Rembrandt was perhaps the greatest portrait painter in European history. His legacy lives on in several museums in Amsterdam. His house in the city, where he worked for 20 years, displays a collection of his etchings among other exhibits. The State Museum is the pearl of Dutch museums, holding the crème-de-la-crème of the 16th- and 17th century Dutch Masters. Rembrandt's works are prominently displayed along with those of Franz Hals, Jan Steen and others. The Museum of Modern Art has an excellent permanent collection of modern artworks and frequently displays traveling exhibits from around the world.

The Van Gogh Museum contains a vast collection of artworks by the renowned Dutch artist. Nearly 700 of his works are represented, including his paintings and drawings. Works of his contemporaries are also displayed here, as well as traveling exhibits of temporary shows of 19th and 20th century artists.

The Leidseplein is the center of Amsterdam's nightlife, which is internationally known for its permissiveness. Brown cafés dot the city, and are a wonderful way to meet the typically friendly Dutch. They are so named for the color of their interiors, darkened over the years from copious amounts of tobacco smoke. Hard drugs are prohibited in Amsterdam, despite a reputation to the contrary. Small amounts of soft drugs such as marijuana are tolerated in the brown cafés and coffee shops.

Amsterdam has many beautiful churches. Dutch sovereigns are crowned at the New Church, which is ironically one of the oldest buildings in the city. The Old Church is, however, aptly named; the building dates from the 13th century and was dedicated to St. Nicholas, the patron saint of Amsterdam.

The Trivia

Fact: Amsterdam is built upon pilings driven into the marshy land. These pilings do not rot, however, because there is so little oxygen in the ground. Houses are built to lean against others for support. Homeowners are taxed according to the number of pilings needed to support their houses; as a result, the thrifty Dutch tend to build rather narrow houses.

Fact: One of the city's cultural attractions is its infamous Red Light District, where prostitution is legal. Unfamiliar tourists are often surprised to see women displayed in windows, offering their services to passersby.

Fact: Beer was first brewed at the Heineken Brewery in the 16th century and continued uninterrupted until 1988. Brewery tours and beer sampling are available.

Why Amsterdam Is a *50 plus one* City

Amsterdam is beautiful and welcoming, tolerant and diverse. The city's history is reflected throughout the metropolitan area. Amsterdam is an engineering marvel that has kept the North Sea at bay for centuries. Thoroughly modern, the city's intimate feel attracts visitors from all over the world.

3

Athens, Greece

The Basic Facts

The capital of Greece, Athens is renowned the world over for its history and importance to Western culture. It is the cultural, economic, governmental and educational center of Greek life. Unfortunately, much of its former glory has been replaced with modern architecture, leading many people to refer to contemporary Athens as a concrete jungle.

Geography

Athens lies at 38 degrees north latitude and 23 degrees 38 minutes longitude. It is located in the plane of Attica and surrounded by mountains, the highest of which is Mount Parnitha, at nearly 5,000 feet. The highest point in Athens, which covers roughly 15 square miles, is the pine-covered Lykavitos Hill.

Climate

The weather in Athens is generally mild, pleasant, and frequently sunny—the ideal tourist environment. Annual temperatures range from the mid-50s Fahrenheit in winter to the mid-90s in summer. Regrettably, the surrounding mountains prevent winds from reaching Athens, and so urban pollution can be problematic in the summer. In fact, the city's pollution is generally considered the worst in Europe

Government

Athens is one of 54 towns and villages that have been subsumed into the Municipality of Athens. A mayor and several district councils govern the municipality. The city itself is divided into seven districts that administer their respective city services.

Demographics

Nearly a third of the entire population of Greece calls Athens home. The population of the city Athens is estimated at 750,000, although the metropolitan area has some 3.2 million inhabitants. More than half of the population is between the ages of 15 and 64, and nearly all residents are ethnic Greeks. Greek Orthodox Christianity is the dominant religion.

Economy

Athens has a mixed capitalist economy and is one of the poorest countries in the European Union. Reconstructing the economy and reducing unemployment are currently the city's major challenges. Tourism and shipping are the main industries of Athens. The city welcomes millions of tourists every year, and its shipping sector is one of the most important in the world. Agriculture accounts for a mere 15 percent of the economy.

The History

Athens is named for Athena, the Greek goddess of wisdom. It is unclear when the city was actually founded. It is known, however, that the Greeks occupied Attica as early as 1900 B.C.; Attica became one of the first Peloponnesian city-states. Royalty was replaced by democracy in 510 B.C. with the creation of an unwritten constitution. The 2 century Golden Age of Greece followed; at this time Athens became a center of culture and intellectualism, which led to the advent of Western civilization.

Athens lost its political leadership in the Peleponnesus after its defeat in the war against its rival city-state Sparta. By the Byzantine era, Athens was little more than an insignificant provincial town. In 1458 A.D the city fell to the Ottoman Empire led by Sultan Mehmet the Conqueror. Ironically, the conquest proved beneficial to the preservation of the city's ruins; the sultan declared that they were to be left unspoiled. The Parthenon, for example, was spared after being converted to a mosque.

By the 17th century, the Ottoman Empire began to fail, and the ancient buildings of Athens were once again neglected. The Venetians laid siege to the city in the late 17th century, and the famed Parthenon was largely destroyed by enemy attack.

The Ottomans relinquished control of Greece in the mid-19th century, and Athens became the capital of the new kingdom, despite the fact that the population now languished at a mere 5,000 inhabitants. The city flourished after being rebuilt in a neoclassical style, and its population grew. As evidence of the city's return to prominence, Athens hosted the first modern Olympics in 1896.

Italy and Germany occupied the city during World War II. Athens was an open city, meaning that it would neither fortify nor attempt to defend itself without risking massive destruction. Soon after the war, archaeologists and preservationists began considerable efforts to restore and protect the city's ancient buildings. Their work has contributed to the city's current blend of modern and ancient architecture.

In anticipation of hosting the Summer Olympics in 2004, Greece overhauled many parts of the city, constructed new housing, improved its public transportation system, expanded its airport, and built state-of-the-art facilities for athletes.

The Sights and Sounds

Although Athens is a sprawling city, most of the key sights and sounds can be found in its compact city center. The Acropolis is the focal point of Athens, a rather flat hill crowned by the Parthenon. The imposing structure has a magnificent presence regardless of the time of day. Even before its completion in 438 B.C., the building was considered a marvel of sophisticated art and architecture. Its original red and blue decorations are long gone, however, and the marble pillars have lost their shine. The largest surviving relic of the original frieze is now in London's British Museum, and Greece has been petitioning for its return for some time.

The National Archaeological Museum displays an extensive collection of antiquities, including the world's largest collection of Greek art and artifacts. The collection at the Goulandris Museum of Cycladic and Greek Ancient Art spans nearly 5,000 years of art history; 100 exhibits date to 3000 B.C. The Acropolis Museum has a significant number of koria, female figures that were sculpted in dedication to Athena. The Byzantine Museum, housed in a 19th century mansion, is dedicated solely to preserving the Byzantine history of Athens and the surrounding area. Religious icons accent models of Greek Byzantine churches, constructed as they might have appeared in their prime.

The Odeon of Herod Atticus is a restored 2nd century Greek theatre built into a hillside; the theatre continues to stage performances. Panathenaic Stadium is a recreation of the ancient Roman stadium building in Athens. This 80,000 seat venue of marble gleams in the bright sun and was built for the 1896 Olympics. Hadrian's Arch was built in 131 to commemorate Roman control of Athens. Constitution Square was built in 1838 as the new royal palace when the Greeks finally separated themselves from the Ottomans; today it is the home of Parliament. The transit station in the square displays fragments and artifacts recovered during construction.

The modern section of Athens also offers several reasons to visit including the shopping center between Omonia Square and Constitution Square. Stores and fine restaurants abound, and trolleys are available from Omonia Square for tourists with tired feet. The Plaka is one of the most popular tourist districts; its neoclassical buildings and traditional tavernas make it one of the most beautiful neighborhoods in the city center. The nightlife of Athens is also a draw; most bars and nightclubs are open until 3 a.m. Betika is a uniquely Greek form of the blues, enjoyed by many. The Psiri neighborhood is the hot new club area with the latest music and dance.

The Trivia

Fact: The Greeks built Athens on and around a large rocky hill with a flat top. This became known as the Acropolis, from the Greek akro (high) and polis (city). The Acropolis gradually became a center of temples and public buildings; ruins of these structures remain to this day.

Fact: The Parthenon has an interesting history. At various times it was a Roman brothel, a Christian Church, a Turkish mosque, and a storage depot for gunpowder.

Why Athens Is a *50 plus one* City

Thousands of years of Greek, Roman and Byzantine culture, art and architecture are represented in Athens. No European city has had a greater influence on Western culture, civilization, and democracy.

4

Auckland, New Zealand

The Basic Facts

Auckland is the largest city in New Zealand and is nicknamed the City of Sails. The city is a combination of well-preserved historical buildings and modern architecture.

Geography

Auckland lies at 36 degrees 53 minutes south latitude and 174 degrees 45 minutes east longitude. Auckland covers 419 square miles along the Hauraki Gulf of the Pacific Ocean and is one of the few world cities to have harbors on two bodies of water. Auckland is located in the North Island of New Zealand.

Climate

Winters in Auckland are cool and damp, while its summers are warm and humid. Annual temperatures range from the mid-50s Fahrenheit in winter to the low 80s Fahrenheit in summer. Because Auckland is located south of the equator, the winter and summer months are opposite from those in the northern hemisphere; winter occurs between June and August, and summer occurs between December and February.

Government

Auckland is governed by a mayor and city council. In 1989 the center city was merged with other areas to form a new Auckland City.

Demographics

The population of metropolitan Auckland is roughly 1.3 million, most of whom speak English. Auckland's transportation systems have not met the needs of its residents, a typical consequence of urban sprawl. Nearly one in seven people are of Maori descent, giving Auckland a significant Polynesian population.

Economy

Tourism and the service industry are important factors in the city's economy. Auckland's trade industry deals in sheep, timber and dairy, and most of New Zealand's shipping and manufacturing is centered in Auckland.

The History

The Auckland region was settled by Maoris around A.D. 450. The area was hotly contested for hundreds of years by groups vying for its rich surrounding lands. In fact, the region's initial name was Tamaki, which in Maori means battle.

European explorers began to visit New Zealand in the late 1700s, and by the end of the century seal and whale hunters and traders took advantage of the area's natural riches. Many were former British convicts from the penal colony in nearby Sydney; as a result, early New Zealand and the Auckland area were lawless and uncivilized frontiers.

Decades of fierce intertribal conflict made for an easy conquest by the European settlers, and by 1840 the British had a firm grasp on the area. Captain William Hobson, New Zealand's first governor, named Auckland the country's capital in honor of Lord Auckland, Hobson's patron and past commander.

Although the South Island flourished immediately after colonization, settlers on the North Island, including the Auckland area, experienced mounting tensions with the Maori. From 1845 to 1872 the New Zealand Wars pitted the British colonists against the Maori; the British prevailed and the Maori leaders withdrew to a remote area of North Island.

The Great Depression of the 1930s devastated the country's economy and led to the rise of the Labour Party, which promised work and social programs to free the city from the economic disaster. Auckland's economy revived somewhat during World War II, when New Zealand troops fought alongside the Allies; the country also aligned with the United Nations in the Korean War and with the United States and its allies in the Vietnam War.

The Sights and Sounds

Acacia Cottage dates from the 1840s and is one of the oldest wooden houses in the city. The cottage is in Cornwall Park in the heart of the city center. Highwic House, built mid-19th century, is a timber Gothic-style period home filled with antique furniture, paintings and all the trappings of the good life. The Auckland Town Hall was built in the early 20th century, an Italianate building quite different from the rest of Auckland's architecture. The building's two large halls are regularly used for concerts and other public events.

A popular modern attraction is the 1,066-foot-tall Sky Tower, built in 1997. The tower has a hotel and casino, a revolving restaurant, and observation decks for a fine view of the city. Adventurous tourists with strong stomachs can try sky jumping—with a harness, of course.

The New Zealand National Maritime Museum contains a large collection of historical maritime artifacts. The museum gives visitors a sense of the importance of ocean trade and sport in the life of the city. The War Memorial Museum is dedicated to the memory of the New Zealand Wars between the settlers and the Maori; the museum's collection includes a variety of Maori arts and crafts. The Auckland Art Gallery is the city's largest permanent collection of paintings by international artists; it is housed in a classic Victorian building.

Auckland Harbour Bridge, built in the 1950s, spans Waitemata Harbour and connects the city to the Hauraki Gulf. The Grafton Bridge that spans Grafton Gully is an engineering wonder of the early 20th century. It was constructed of reinforced concrete, and when completed it was the world's largest single-span bridge.

The metropolitan area has more than 100 marvelous beaches, where visitors can sunbathe, swim, scuba, snorkel and surf. The beaches closest to the city center are the East Coast beaches located on Tamaki Drive. Nearby are a host of restaurants, cafés and pubs, along with family-friendly playgrounds and open spaces.

The Auckland Botanic Gardens are south of the city center and offer a sampling of New Zealand's natural beauty. The vast collection of plants includes exotics generally unknown to visitors from the northern hemisphere. Also here are delightfully landscaped green spaces, fountains and walking paths, some of the finest in New Zealand.

One of the most exciting and invigorating ways to see Auckland and the North Island of New Zealand is a balloon trip over the city. Trips leave daily from the Albany district of Auckland, and a champagne toast is included. If terra firma is more your style, take a tour of the city's northeastern coastline aboard one of the many cruise ships. Tour guides provide commentary on the city and its history, and some voyages include meals. Cruises are scheduled throughout the day and into the evening.

The Trivia

Fact: In 1984 New Zealand banned from its ports all ships carrying nuclear weapons or powered by nuclear fuel. This policy led to a contentious situation with the United States, after a naval destroyer was denied access to a port; U.S.

officials refused to say whether the vessel's cargo included nuclear weapons. As a result of the dispute, the United States suspended its obligations under the ANZUS treaty, a military alliance between Australia, New Zealand, and the United States.

Why Auckland Is a *50 plus one* City

Auckland has an idyllic location, and the physical beauty of the land and surrounding sea are compelling to any first-time visitor. Simply to visit Auckland is an event, as it is so far from the big cities of Europe and North America.

5

Bangkok, Thailand

The Basic Facts

Bangkok is the capital of Thailand and is the country's largest city. It is still known as the Venice of the East, although most of the city's canals have now been replaced with paved roads.

Geography

Bangkok lies at 13 degrees 50 minutes north latitude and 100 degrees 29 minutes east longitude. The city is located in the delta of the Great Chao Phraya River near the Gulf of Thailand, in the heart of Thailand's agricultural region.

Climate

Bangkok has a tropical monsoon climate and is considered one of the hottest urban centers in the world. The city swelters in a humid environment where the temperature rarely departs from the high 80s and lower 90s Fahrenheit. Bangkok receives a considerable amount of rain during the monsoon season, especially in September, when the area receives up to a foot of rain.

Government

Bangkok is one of two special administrative areas in Thailand in which citizens vote for their governor. Urban sprawl in recent years led to the merger of the provinces of Bangkok and Thonburi province. The city is divided into 50 administrative districts.

Demographics

The population of the metropolitan area is estimated at a staggering nine million people, with about six million people living in Bangkok itself. The city is known for its infamous traffic jams, despite the creation of new light rail and subway lines. More than half of Bangkok residents claim Chinese ancestry, and the city has sizable numbers of European and American expatriates.

Economy

Bangkok is a leading commercial center of Thailand and the entire Southeast Asian region. Food processing, lumber and wood products, and textiles are important manufacturers, followed closely by rice milling, oil and shipbuilding. Bangkok's manmade harbor handles most of Thailand's commercial goods. The city is the hub of the continental Southeast Asian railway, and a network of modern highways advances its economic position. The city's canal system permits the inexpensive and efficient transportation of goods.

The History

Bangkok began as a small trading center and port community originally called Bang Makok, or City of Olives in a primitive Thai dialect. Thailand fought a lengthy war with neighboring Burma in the late 18th century, after which Bangkok fell to Burma.

King Rama I, the first monarch of the Chakri Dynasty, founded modern Bangkok in 1782. The King gave Bangkok a 21-word name that is commonly abbreviated (thank goodness!) as Krung Thep, meaning City of Angels. Although Bangkok is only one district in Krung Thep, most foreigners refer to the city by its more familiar name.

The city was designed in accordance with the Thai belief that the king's palace is the center of the universe. The Grand Palace was the first building to be constructed, and major temples and government structures were built nearby. Housing and other less-important buildings were relegated to areas far from the palace.

Bangkok experienced explosive growth in the 1990s; today it is a national and regional center for trade, tourism and government. The city's rapid growth came with a price, however; nearly one-sixth of the city's housing is located in slums that suffer greatly from inadequate garbage collection. Bangkok's high population density has led to constant traffic jams and air pollution due to vehicle exhaust. The land under the city has been sinking up to four inches a year for decades, and the city suffers from frequent floods, especially during the rainy season. Even so, modern Bangkok is an intriguing blend of old buildings and cutting-edge new construction.

The Sights and Sounds

Millions of world travelers visit Bangkok each year, for business and for pleasure. The city abounds with exotic sights and sounds. The Grand Palace, built in 1782, is a truly amazing building that covers some 53 acres of land. The palace is a complex of buildings, each dedicated to a specific role: a religious temple; a ceremonial complex; the royal residence and guest area; and staff and government offices.

The National Museum is the largest in Southeast Asia and was originally part of the Grand Palace. Its collection focuses on the whole of Thai history and exhibits many prehistoric artifacts. The Red House is an 18th century traditional Thai building decorated in all the splendor of the period: elephant chairs, royal emblems, wood carvings, magnificent statues of Buddha, jewelry, ceramics and religious artifacts.

Wat Phra Kaew, part of the Grand Palace, is the Temple of the Emerald Buddha and the shrine that is most revered by the people of Bangkok. The focal point is the statue itself, two feet tall atop an enormous gold base. It is said to have been carved in the 14th century.

The National Museum of the Royal Barges provides a fascinating glimpse into Thai history and culture. Thailand began as an agricultural society with settled communities near the waterways, and the river was an important means of transport and communication. Many of the country's finest historical barges are here, including:

- The Suphannahong Royal Barge, its prow resembling a mythological swan. The vessel was completed in the reign of King Rama VI, is the highest class of Royal Barge, and was awarded the Sea Heritage Medal from the World Ships Organization of Great Britain in 1981.
- The Anantanagaraj Royal Barge, its prow carved in the form of a Naga, a seven-headed figure. This barged carried the statue of Buddha during festivals.
- The Anekchartputchong Royal Barge, an elaborately-painted vessel built during the reign of King Rama V.

Bangkok has more than 300 Buddhist temples; two deserve special mention and should not be missed. Wat Po, or the Temple of the Reclining Buddha, was built in the 16th century and is the largest temple in Bangkok. The main attraction is the statue itself, a staggering 150 feet long and covered in gold leaf. Wat Arun, the Temple of the Dawn, was originally a royal chapel. This temple has a stunning 282-foot-tall tower and its exterior is clad in multi-color ceramics from throughout Thailand.

Curious and adventurous tourists visit Patpong. This area is not only well known for its sex bars and night market, but also for its assortment of shops that specialize in black-market goods. A more respectable and trendy nighttime spot is along Sukhumvit Road, where one can find top bars and clubs.

The Trivia

Fact: A modern business and commercial district has developed over the last few years about three miles from the Grand Palace. This area is a major tourist attraction and contains office buildings, shops, nightclubs and movie theaters.

Fact: Bangkok avoided the catastrophic damage and incomprehensible loss of life following the tsunami that overwhelmed Southeast Asia in late December 2004. Its location beyond the Malay Peninsula spared the city from the ocean's wrath.

Fact: Bangkok's official full name is Krungthep Maha Nakorn Amorn Ratanakosindra Mahindrayudhya Mahadilokpop Noporatana Rajthani Burirom Udom Rajnivet Mahastan Amorn Rimarn Avatarn Satit Sakkatuttiya Vishnukarm Prasit (whew!). The rough English translation is the city of angels, the great city, the eternal jewel city, the impregnable city of God Indra, the grand capital of the world endowed with nine precious gems, the happy city, abounding in an enormous Royal Palace that resembles the heavenly abode where reigns the reincarnated god, a city given by Indra and built by Vishnukarn. The actual translation is unknown even to most Thais, as the name is in an ancient Thai language.

Why Bangkok Is a *50 plus one* City

Bangkok is exotic, dynamic and filled with history and tradition of the Thai people. The city exemplifies the increasing global influence of the Asian economy, which has come into its own in the last 40 years.

6

Barcelona, Spain

The Basic Facts

Barcelona is the capital of the autonomous region of Catalonia in northeast Spain. The city has a rich and romantic history that attracts millions of international tourists every year.

Geography

Barcelona lies at 41 degrees 25 minutes north latitude and 2 degrees 84 minutes east longitude. Barcelona is located on the Mediterranean between the Llobregat and Besòs Rivers, a 2-hour drive from the French border.

Climate

Barcelona has well-defined seasons with high humidity throughout the year. Summers can be quite warm, winter is rather pleasant, but fall and spring are the best times to visit the city. Annual temperatures range from the mid-60s Fahrenheit in winter to the mid-90s Fahrenheit in summer.

Government

Barcelona has a mayor-city council form of government. The Municipal Council is the highest level of political representation for citizens in government; chaired by the mayor and consisting of 41 councillors, the council manages most municipal functions.

Economy

Barcelona is the second largest city in Spain, its largest port, and its chief commercial and industrial center. Manufacturing industries include textiles, machinery, automobiles, locomotives, airplanes, and electrical equipment. International banking and finance are also important to the city's economy.

Demographics

The population of the city of Barcelona is estimated at 1.6 million people. Some 230,000 residents are immigrants from the former Spanish colonies in Latin America; others come from Morocco, Pakistan, Romania, and Ukraine. Barcelona residents use both Catalan and Castillian Spanish.

The History

Barcelona was founded in 230 B.C. by the Carthaginians. Over the next 1,000 years the city was repeatedly invaded, notably by the Visigoths in the early 5th century and by the Moors in the 8th century. Barcelona's modern age began in 801 A.D., when armies from what would become France conquered the city and defeated the Moors. A succession of counts governed Barcelona from the 9th to the 12th centuries, when the city developed into an important commercial and industrial center. Barcelona later united with Aragon and became the capital of the region known as Catalonia.

During the 14th century, Barcelona ruled a small empire that included Sicily, Malta, Sardinia, Valencia, the Balearics, and parts of France and Greece. This empire collapsed by the 15th century, however, and the Catalans united with the nearby region of Castille. The rulers of Castille and Aragon looted Barcelona's city coffers to fund their imperial ambitions, reducing the city's importance in the region. To add insult to injury, Barcelona was prevented from trading with the newly-discovered Americas.

After Catalonia fell in 1714, Philip V, the French contender for the Spanish throne, demolished a huge section of the La Ribera (the merchants' quarter) and erected the Ciutadella. Philip was hated by his subjects, and so he watched over them from this large fort. He forbade use of the Catalan language and closed the city's university.

Catalonia finally gained permission to trade with the Americas in 1778. Spain's first industrial revolution began in Barcelona and focused on cotton manufacturing. The city was later occupied by French forces during the Napoleonic Wars. Since then it has remained under Spanish control.

During the mid-19th century Barcelona once again became a hotbed of discontent and was the center of many revolts against the Spanish monarchy. The city was the seat of the Republican government during the Spanish Civil War against the Fascist forces of General Francisco Franco. Barcelona fell to Franco in 1939 and many Catalonians fled to France or Andorra. The Spanish monarchy was re-established after Franco's death, and Barcelona regained its status as a center of culture and trade. Barcelona hosted the 1992 Summer Olympics.

The Sights and Sounds

Barcelona, at 2,000 years old, rivals Madrid as the cultural, architectural and entertainment capital of Spain. Barcelona grew and thrived at a time when Madrid was barely on the map. Barcelona is an overwhelming Catholic city and has a number of spectacular churches. The Catedral de la Seu is a symbol of local pride. It was constructed over the course of 2 centuries and completed in 1450, although parts of the church were added as late as 1892. The Lepanto Chapel within the church is highly prized by local residents. Many visitors relish Santa Maria del Mar for its wonderful 14th century Gothic architecture; most locals consider it the finest church in all of Barcelona. The Temple Expiatori de la Sagrada Familia, designed by the famous architect Antonio Gaudi, displays the history of Christianity on its façade. It remains under construction, but when finished the complex will include 18 towers.

The National Museum of Catalan Art offers a wealth of Romanesque and Gothic art from around the area. The Miro Foundation was a gift to the city from its famous son, Joan Miró; not surprisingly, many of his works are prominently displayed in the museum's exhibit halls. The Museu Picasso is housed in two 15th century buildings and houses an extensive collection of the artist's early works, including those from the Rose Period and the Blue Period.

Casa Mila is a popular home that was designed by Gaudi; its curving façade seems to slither around the block like a snake. The site also contains a museum dedicated to Gaudi's architectural creations. Famous examples of late 19th century architecture and style can be found in the area of the city called Eixample, which is also where the city's most elegant shops and cafes are to be found. The district is particularly prized for its Spanish version of Art Nouveau buildings and design.

Bullfighting is a traditional spectator sport in Barcelona that remains popular with locals despite its controversial nature. Events are held on Sundays between March and October at the Monumental; the arena also has a museum dedicated to the sport.

Evenings in Barcelona often stretch into the wee hours of the morning. The city is chock-full of cafes, cabarets, champagne bars, discos, jazz clubs and more. The many restaurants called tapas bars offer a variety of delightful dishes. Do not miss the flamenco dancers for a true sense of local culture.

The Trivia

Fact: During the 19th century Barcelona was the nexus of the Catalan Renaissance, a crusade by poets, writers and other artists to popularize Catalan as the people's language.

Fact: According to tradition, Christopher Columbus announced his discovery of the New World in Barcelona's Plaza del Rey.

Fact: Barcelona was a pioneer of early European education. The University of Barcelona, founded in 1450, continues to be a well-respected academic institution.

Why Barcelona Is a *50 plus one* City

Barcelona may not be the capital of Spain, but is the country's focal point of culture, literature, and architecture. Few cities in the world can match the richness and the complexity that make up modern Barcelona.

7

Beijing, China

The Basic Facts

Beijing is the capital of the People's Republic of China and is the country's second largest city. The city is a regional center for politics, education, and culture, and will be the site of the 2008 Summer Olympics.

Geography

Beijing lies at 33 degrees 55 minutes north latitude and 116 degrees 23 minutes east longitude. The city is located the North China plain, 100 miles inland from the Bo Gulf, and shielded by mountains to north, northwest and west. Beijing's two main rivers are the Yongding and the Chaobai.

Climate

Beijing's weather can be harsh at any time of year. Annual temperatures range from the low 20s Fahrenheit in winter to the low 80s Fahrenheit in summer. Humidity is high in summer and low in winter, and causes the temperatures to feel more extreme than they actually are. Beijing suffers from significant air pollution and seasonal dust storms; the former as a result of poorly regulated manufacturing industries, and the latter from desert erosion in northern China.

Government

Beijing is one of four direct-controlled municipalities in the country, and has the same political status as a Chinese province. The city is divided into 18 county-level divisions and further subdivided into 273 township-level divisions.

Demographics

Nearly all Beijing residents are native Chinese of Han ethnicity; other ethnic groups represented include Manchu, Mongol and Hui. There has been an influx of South Korean immigrants to the city in recent years, primarily students and international expatriates involved in global commerce. Mandarin Chinese, the country's official language, is the primary language used in the city. The metropolitan area population is estimated to be 15 million.

Economy

Beijing's economic boom of the late 20th century continues today, especially in the high-tech, real estate, and automobile sectors. As China's capital city, government entities in Beijing are major employers. Other important industries in the metropolitan area include finance, banking, construction, and trades.

The History

The history of modern-day Beijing dates to the 13th century, when the Mongol forces of Kublai Khan invaded the city. The Khan declared Beijing as his capital city, a strategic move considering that the city is roughly 300 miles from the Mongolian border. Various dynasties over the next 3 centuries altered the face of Beijing by adding their own temples, palaces and other buildings.

China remained relatively isolated from the West until the late 19th century, when France and Britain forced the country to allow foreign diplomats into Beijing. This decision caused discontent among Chinese nationalists, and at the turn of the 20th century the bloody Boxer Rebellion attempted to expel Westerners from China. Western nations attacked Beijing in response and destroyed much of the city. In the decade following the rebellion, Republican sympathizers severely criticized the existing Qing Dynasty. In 1912 their discontent culminated with the creation of the Republic of China and the end of 2 centuries of Chinese dynastic rule.

In 1928 Chiang Kai-Shek became the leader of the Republic of China, after successfully ousting the warlords that had controlled the republic since its inception. The emerging Chinese Communist Party (CCP) gained in power after World War II, and in 1949 the country became known as the People's Republic of China. Its leader was Mao Zedong, the head of the CCP, who later named Beijing as the capital of the country. In the 1960s the student-dominated Red Guard purged the Chinese Communists of any opposition to Mao's policies and replaced the existing Beijing government with a revolutionary committee.

In 1989 Beijing's Tiananmen Square, in front of the Forbidden City, was the site of a large pro-democracy protest against the Chinese government. A famous image from that protest is that of the Unknown Rebel, a student protester who blocked the path of a series of tanks sent to restore order in the square. Hundreds died and thousands were injured during the ultimately unsuccessful protest that was crushed by the military.

The Sights and Sounds

Beijing is an enigma, a modern city that belies its roots as an imperial stronghold. Westerners refer to it as the Forbidden City even today, although it is officially known as the Palace Museum. The Forbidden City itself is the former home of China's succession of emperors; its ornate buildings, gardens and courtyards cover an area of nearly 178 acres.

Tiananmen Square is at the south edge of the Forbidden City and is framed by the Gate of Heavenly Peace. On Chinese national holidays parades and fireworks are held in the square. Every year, the emperor offered prayers at the Temple of Heaven for a good harvest. Surrounded by a park, the Temple is worth a short visit. In fact, it may seem familiar from seeing it depicted on the wallpaper of Chinese restaurants. Two interesting points are the echo effect inside the temple and the stone at the entrance that amplifies the voice of the person who stands in front of it.

No visitor to China can leave without visiting the Great Wall. Although it is one of the Seven Wonders of the Medieval Mind, today considerable portions of the wall are in serious disrepair. Even so, it is one of the largest and most impressive man-made structures in the world. The Great Wall facilitated information exchange and trade in goods between regions, and also prevented invasion from outsiders.

Tourists can discover a wealth of culinary curiosities as they wander the streets of Beijing. Exotic concoctions at the night markets scattered about the city include skewered insects, seahorses and squid. More familiar Western fare is available, including street food such as dumplings, noodles and skewers of chicken, lamb or beef.

Hot pot, the local specialty, is usually only available in winter. This is essentially a fondue in which meat, vegetables or tofu are seasoned to taste and dipped in hot water. Hot pot is best enjoyed in a large group so that everyone can mix and match ingredients and sauces.

Peking duck is a local delicacy served by most local restaurants; authentic preparation of this dish takes several days. Seek out the Qianmen Quanjude Roast Duck Restaurant near Tiananmen Square. This restaurant, established in 1864, is the locals' choice for this renowned Chinese creation.

The Trivia

Fact: Beijing's houses are generally old and border narrow, tree-lined alleys known as hutongs. Newer housing developments have recently sprung up in suburbs north and northwest of the city.

Fact: The Forbidden City is so named that for many years, only emperors and authorized persons were granted access. The 1987 motion picture *The Last Emperor* was the first to be filmed with the Forbidden City, after having been granted special permission by the Chinese government.

Fact: Beijing will host the 2008 Summer Olympics.

Why Beijing Is a *50 plus one* City

Beijing has survived 2,000 years of foreign invasion, war, and governmental and cultural change to emerge as the symbol of Chinese history and culture. Visitors to this ancient city are often captivated and frequently overwhelmed by its history and its treasures.

8

Berlin, Germany

The Basic Facts

Berlin is the capital and largest city of Germany, and was a focal point during the Cold War of the 20th century. Today the city is a European center for culture, politics and economics.

Geography

Berlin lies at 52 degrees 31 minutes north latitude and 13 degrees 28 minutes east longitude. The metropolitan area covers more than 2,100 square miles in east central Germany, at the confluence of the Spree and Havel Rivers. Berlin is linked to the Baltic Sea by a series of canals and rivers. Government and financial offices are located in the downtown area, while housing developments and industrial firms are located mainly in the outlying areas.

Climate

Annual temperatures in Berlin range from the mid-30s Fahrenheit in winter to the mid-60s Fahrenheit in summer. Although rain is possible year-round, the wettest months are June and August. Winters can sometimes be severe, and are typically cold and dry.

Government

Berlin is comprised 23 administrative districts, governed by a 240-member Abgeordnetenhaus (House of Representatives), which makes the city laws and elects the governing mayor. With House approval, the mayor appoints a deputy mayor and Senat (cabinet) to administer city government. The mayor and representatives serve 4-year terms. Berlin is also one of Germany's 16 states, and city residents elect representatives to the Bundestag (Federal Diet) and the Bundesrat (Federal Council).

Demographics

Native-born Germans constitute nearly 90 percent of Berlin's population. Non-German residents include Turks–the largest concentration outside of Turkey–Greeks, Italians, Poles, Russians, Americans, Asians, and Africans. The metropolitan area population is estimated at 4.2 million.

Economy

Prior to World War II, Berlin was an important German industrial center. The economy's industrial and construction sectors have lagged in recent years, but this deficiency has been overcome by a sharp rise in both government and service jobs. Manufacturing remains an important part of the economy; goods produced include electrical products, chemicals, clothing, processed foods, and machinery.

Berlin is a major German railway hub, and the city has an efficient public transportation system that operates surface rail (S-Bahn, or Schnellbahn), subways (U-Bahn, or Untergrundbahn), trams (Straßenbahn), buses, and ferries. The city's international airport is Tegel International, just outside the city. Berlin-Schönefeld International and Tempelhof serve charter flights and regional flights, respectively.

The History

Berlin was founded in the 12th century, and by the 15th century it had become the capital of the German state of Brandenburg. The city fell into decline in the 17th century due to war and medical epidemics, but under the rule of Frederick William (the Great Elector) the city revived and blossomed into a major trading and cultural center.

In the early 19th century, the city became the capital of Prussia, and later was the center of the German Empire. The Weimer Republic formed following World War I, and Berlin experienced political strife, riots, and strikes. Runaway inflation plagued the republic and the city during this period, leading to the rise of the Nazis in the 1930s and the onset of World War II.

Berlin was devastated by the Allies during World War II. Following Germany's surrender in 1945, the city was divided into sectors, of which Britain, France, the Soviet Union and the United States controlled one each. In 1948, the Soviet Union blocked surface routes to West Berlin, effectively preventing food and other necessary supplies from reaching residents of those sectors. In response, the United States military airlifted countless tons of supplies to West Berlin over 462 days in 1948 and 1949; were it not for this intervention, later known as the Berlin Airlift, untold numbers of West Berliners would have perished from malnutrition and medical neglect.

West Berlin revived as a trade and cultural center while East Berlin languished under its Communist-run government. In 1961, the Soviets constructed the Berlin Wall to stem the tide of East Germans who were fleeing the city. Over the next 28 years, more than 170 people died trying to scale the Wall's barricades and barbed wire. As the Communist government waned in the Soviet Union, East Germany ended travel restrictions between East and West Berlin in 1989. In the weeks that followed, throngs of people exuberantly dismantled the Wall, a historic event that was televised around the world. Communists soon lost control of the East German government, and in 1990 the country was reunited as the Federal Republic of Germany. The German Parliament, which had moved to Bonn during the Cold War, returned to the Reichstag in Berlin in 1999.

The Sights and Sounds

The former divisions of east and west are familiar to visitors and provide a point of reference in locating the city's various tourist attractions.

In the west, begin at the Egyptian Museum of Berlin to see the magnificent 3,300-year old bust of Queen Nefertiti. The Cultural Forum is a complex of cultural jewels including the Museum of Decorative Arts, the Painting Gallery, and the New National Gallery designed by Mies van der Rohe. The Forum is also home to the world-famous Berlin Philharmonic Orchestra. The Dahlem Museum is a four-building campus displaying artifacts from around the world, including art from the early European, Indian and Asian eras.

Contemporary visitors are fascinated by the Brandenburg Gate, the 18th century landmark that is a symbol of peace. The Holocaust Memorial is located just south of this area. The Reichstag (Parliament) opened in 1894 and was originally the parliament building of the German Empire. The Reichstag's destruction by fire in 1933 spurred the rise of the Nazi regime. The building has been restored and is a popular tourist attraction.

For an excellent view of Berlin, climb the steps of the Siegessäule. This memorial known as the Victory Column was erected in 1873 to commemorate Prussia's victory in the Danish Prussian war. Four tunnels lead to the top of the 220-foot-tall and provide a lovely view of the Tiergarten.

Many of Berlin's older historic sites are in the Eastern sections of the city. The Berliner Dom (Cathedral) is a 19th century church known for its large green dome. Many Prussian nobles are laid to rest here. The Hamburger Bahnhof is a beautiful restored 19th century train station; the grand interaction of color, glass and light in the new wing is a must-see. The station also contains a wonderful collection of contemporary public art.

The Old National Gallery and the Old Museum are located on Museum Island in the middle of the Spree River. The National Gallery houses 19th and 20th century paintings and sculptures, and the Old Museum has a vast collection of Greek, Roman and Old German art. The Pergamon Museum is named for its centerpiece, the Pergamon Altar. This outstanding example of ancient Greek architecture dates from the 2nd century B.C. and is 370 feet in length.

Berlin lives up to its reputation as a sophisticated yet naughty environment. There are more than 6,000 pubs, bars and clubs in the city, as well as jazz clubs, theatres, and cabarets for which Berlin is renowned.

The Trivia

Fact: An important cultural center of Berlin is the Mitte, built around Unter den Linden (the boulevard Under the Linden Trees). World-famous museums and art galleries are located in this area.

Fact: Victorious German armies traditionally paraded through the Brandenburg Gate to the delight of well-wishers.

Fact: One of Berlin's major recreation areas is the Grunewald, a forest along the Havel River. The Teufelsberg (Devil's Mountain) is a man-made hill built for climbing and winter sports; it was constructed from the rubble remaining after World War II.

Fact: Portions of the Berlin Wall have been preserved at Potsdamer Platz, in Bernauer Straße, and in the East Side Gallery along the Spree River.

Why Berlin Is a *50 plus one* City

Berlin has outlasted centuries of turmoil and devastation largely because it is a resilient city. Berlin's art and architecture are unmatched in the world, drawing millions of visitors each year to stand in awe of this city's great history.

9

Bombay, India
(Mumbai, India)

The Basic Facts

Bombay (now called Mumbai) is the capital of the state of Maharashtra in India. Following Indian independence, the Bombay State was divided into the Maharashtra and Gujarat states, based upon the majority language of each area; Bombay remained the capital of Maharashtra. In 1996 the city's name was officially changed from Bombay to Mumbai, which is its name in the Marathi language; many non-Indians still refer to it as Bombay.

Geography

Bombay lies at 18 degrees 58 minutes north latitude and 72 degrees 50 minutes east longitude. The city is built on the Salsette Island (made up of seven islands connected by reclaimed land) off the western coast of India. The city is linked to the Indian mainland by several bridges, has a deep natural harbor, and is the fourth most populous metropolitan area in the world. Most of the city is at sea level, with the exception of the hilly northern part of the island. Three lakes are located within Bombay: Tulsi Lake, Vihar Lake and Powai Lake.

Climate

Bombay lies in the tropical zone and its climate reflects that fact. Spring and summer are typically humid, while fall and winter are typically dry. Temperatures depend largely on humidity; average temperatures range from the lower 50s Fahrenheit in winter to over 100 degrees Fahrenheit in summer. The monsoons that drench Bombay from June to September provide most of the city's annual rainfall.

Government

Bombay is separated into two districts, each under the jurisdiction of a District Collector. The Collectors are responsible for property records, tax collection and election administration.

The Brihanmumbai Municipal Corporation (BMC) administers the city's government departments and infrastructure. Executive power is held by the Municipal Commissioner, who is appointed by the state government. The BMC consists of 227 directly-elected Councilors, who represent each of the city's 24 municipal wards, and five nominated Councilors. Each ward also has an Assistant Municipal Commissioner to direct administrative services. The role of the city mayor is largely ceremonial.

Demographics

Most Bombay residents are native Maharashtrians and speak the state's official language of Marathi. However, the city reflects much of the overall flavor of India, with minority groups from every part of the country. Hindus constitute the largest religious group in Bombay, although smaller numbers of Muslims, Christians, Buddhists, and others live in the city. Hindi is the language spoken by most residents. The total population is estimated to be more than 12 million.

Economy

Many banks and insurance companies are located in Bombay, making it a major Indian financial center. The port and trade industries are prevalent and employ many residents. The city's industries produce goods such as cotton textiles, leather articles and transportation equipment. Bombay is also the center of Bollywood, India's thriving film and television industry.

The History

Bombay was originally an archipelago of seven islands. Undocumented evidence suggests that the area may have been inhabited since the Stone Age. More credible information points to human habitation as far back as 250 B.C. Until 1534 the islands were controlled by local rulers, when the Portuguese took the islands by force and founded what would become modern Bombay. In 1662 Portugal gave the islands to English King Charles II as a dowry for his marriage to the Portuguese royal Catherine of Braganza. The British East India Company later leased the islands to construct a major port. The port was so successful that in 1687 Bombay became the company's headquarters. The British warded off several attempts by Indian nationalists to retake the islands over the next 100 years. British governors of the city reinforced its defenses and constructed numerous bridges to the mainland.

In 1817 a major civil engineering project began that would unite the island archipelago into a single land mass. This project, completed in 1845, was known as the Hornby Vellard after William Hornby, Governor of Bombay.

Bombay became the center of the Indian independence movement in the 1940s, including the All India Congress Committee sessions of 1942. The movement eventually ended British control of the country, and in August, 1947 India formally declared its independence.

The Sights and Sounds

Visitors may initially view Bombay as a chaotic, overwhelming city. Indeed, traffic congestion is the rule, and the city teems with people rushing here are there. After a while, however, one grows accustomed to the hum of the city. In recent years, many monuments and tourist attractions have been renamed in an attempt to downplay their colonial British origins. Nevertheless, most locals still know them by their English names. In most cases, visitors should not have much difficulty finding their way around.

After the Taj Mahal, the Gateway of India is the country's most recognizable structures. Construction of this 85-foot-tall monument began in 1911 and it commemorates the first visit of King George and Queen Mary to Bombay. This monument is beautiful from a distance, but to see its architectural details requires a closer look. The Gateway is located in South Bombay and is a good place to enjoy people watching against the backdrop of the nearby waterfront. A variety of boat trips are available just across the street. Just a few miles across the water from the Gateway of India are the Elephanta Caves, which contain many centuries-old rock carvings and sculptures.

The Prince of Wales Museum houses a large assortment of Indian and Asian artifacts; visitors need more than one day to see the entire collection. Of special interest are the statues of the gods located in a gallery off the main entrance.

Mani Bhavan Ghandi Sangrahalaya is a modest home on Laburnum Road where Mohandas K. (Mahatma) Gandhi stayed while visiting Bombay. It is the former home of his friend Shri Revashankar Jhaveri and is now an important museum chronicling the life of the renowned spiritual leader. Gandhi's room on the second floor appears as it was when he last visited, and visitors can view the room from behind a glass partition. Scholars will marvel at the large collection of Gandhi's papers as well as numerous books and materials about him.

The Jehangir Art Gallery, adjacent to the Prince of Wales Museum, is a popular tourist attraction. The gallery's exhibits include photographs and oils by nationally-recognized Indian artists.

Chhatrapati Shivaji Terminus (formerly Victoria Terminus) is a historic railway station that looks more like a Gothic museum. This building was completed in 1888 and its architecture blends Gothic and Indian influences. The station is still in operation and is one of the busiest rail stations in the country.

The Trivia

Fact: The name Bombay is derived from the Portuguese Bom Bahia. The inhabitants referred to the area as Mumba, after a Hindu deity.

Fact: One of the more famous Bombay landmarks is the Parsi Tower of Silence on Malabar Hill. They were constructed in the 17th century by the Zoroastrians (Parsis). Adherents of this religion consider dead bodies to be unclean. They therefore place corpses atop the towers, and later throw the bones into an ossuary pit.

Fact: In April 1944 a mysterious fire caused the explosion of the cargo ship Fort Stikine in the harbor. Following the explosion, two million British pounds' worth of gold bars literally rained from the skies. Most were recovered and returned to the British government.

Why Bombay Is a *50 plus one* City

Bombay represents the pride and spirit of India. It showcases the rise in both political and economic influence of the new India. No other city in India has quite the same combination of colonial and Indian influences as Bombay. It is a thoroughly modern Indian city, rich with Indian culture, traditions and history.

10

Boston, United States

The Basic Facts

Boston is the capital and largest city in the Commonwealth of Massachusetts. It is the unofficial capital of the region known as New England and one of the oldest, wealthiest, and most culturally significant U.S. cities.

Geography

Boston lies at 42 degrees 15 minutes north latitude and 71 degrees 7 minutes west longitude. The city covers approximately 90 square miles—46 percent of which is water—in east-central Massachusetts. Boston is 19 feet above sea level at its highest point, and much of the Back Bay and South End sections are built on reclaimed land. The Charles River separates Boston proper from Cambridge, Watertown, and Charlestown.

Climate

The weather in Boston changes rapidly; it is not uncommon for the city to experience 50-degree temperature swings over the course of several days. Summers are typically warm and humid, and winters are often cold and windy, although Boston has experienced snow in October and unseasonable warmth in February. Annual temperatures range from the mid-30s Fahrenheit in winter to the low 80s Fahrenheit in summer.

Government

Boston has a strong mayor form of government, in which the mayor is vested with extensive executive powers. The mayor is elected to a 4-year term by plurality voting. The Boston city council is elected every 2 years.

Demographics

The population of the city of Boston is approximately 590,000. The metropolitan area, encompassing parts of New Hampshire, Maine, Rhode Island, and

Connecticut, has a population of 5.8 million. The largest ethnic group in the city is undoubtedly those of Irish descent, and thus makes Boston the unofficial capital of Irish America.

Economy

Boston's has a diversified economic base; important sectors include finance, health care, education, insurance, biotechnology, and business services. Area universities are among the finest in the United States and have a significant impact in the city's economy. Boston is home to a major port. The major airport in Boston is Logan International, located in the East Boston neighborhood. First-time visitors to Boston often carp about finding their way around the city, for many reasons: the streets are largely devoid of a structured numbering system; street names change often; and roundabouts confound disoriented drivers. Boston's public transportation system is popular with those who prefer not to navigate the city on their own. The system includes buses, water shuttles, commuter rail, and a subway—the first of its kind in the United States.

The History

The area of present-day Boston was originally settled by the Massachusett Indians and inhabited by a variety of indigenous groups who called the area Shawmut. The first European settlers arrived in Boston in 1630; these were the Puritans, who initially named the area Trimountaine. The city was renamed Boston after the city of the same name in Lincolnshire, England.

In 1629 the Puritans, led by John Winthrop, signed the Cambridge Agreement to ensure self-governance for Boston and the Massachusetts Bay Colony. This Christian sect was known for its religious devotion, and had a definite impact on the history of early Boston. At the time, the city was said to have a special relationship with God; it was known as the City on the Hill to reference to its closeness to Heaven. Boston became the capital of the Massachusetts Bay Colony in the 1630s, and only Puritans could vote or hold public office.

Puritan Boston was a strict but stable environment in which education was emphasized. The first school in America, Boston's Latin School, was founded in 1635, and Harvard College was founded in the next year. Boston schools became the model for modern education, and the city eventually became one of the great centers of learning in the United States.

In the 1700s Boston grew rapidly and gradually abolished most strict Puritan laws. In the 1770s, however, Boston came into conflict with the British government, which attempted to exert direct control and taxation on the American colonies.

Many events leading up to and part of the American Revolution occurred in Boston: the Boston Massacre; the Boston Tea Party; Paul Revere's midnight ride; and the early Revolutionary battles of Bunker Hill, Lexington and Concord, and the Siege of Boston.

After the Revolutionary War, Boston's economy thrived with the growth of foreign trade, and by the mid-1800s manufacturing became the dominant economic sector. Boston became known as a center for literature, the arts, and the Abolitionist movement.

Boston's once-thriving industry began to show its age at the turn of the 20th century, and the city lost many jobs as a result. In the 1970s urban renewal laid the foundation for the new city of Boston. During the 1980s the city earned a national reputation for its resistance to busing and school integration. New service businesses replaced the old manufacturing base, and once again Boston is an economically vibrant city. Boston recently completed a massive public works project, the construction of a tunnel designed to ease traffic congestion; Bostonians nicknamed the project the Big Dig.

The Sights and Sounds

The Boston National Historical Park is located in the downtown area, and contains buildings and areas that figured prominently during the American Revolution. The three-mile Freedom Trail passes many of these sites, as well as Boston Common and the Boston Public Garden. Locals enjoy ice-skating on the Frog Pond at Boston Common during the winter. The Esplanade is a popular park along the banks of the Charles River.

Landmarks in Boston's Back Bay district include the Boston Public Library, Copley Square, and Newbury Street. The historic John Hancock Building still stands today, although the company's offices are currently located in an adjacent modern building.

Notable museums in the city are the Museum of Fine Arts, the Gardner Museum, and the Museum of Science. The University of Massachusetts is a short distance away and has a children's museum, aquarium, and zoo, as well as the Boston Athenaeum, one of the oldest independent libraries in the country.

Bostonians love their sports, and sporting events always draw large crowds. The Boston Bruins of the National Hockey League and the Boston Celtics of the National Basketball Association share their home at TD Banknorth Garden. Historic Fenway Park, which opened in 1912, is the home of the Boston Red Sox. Fenway is home to the imposing Green Monster, the 37-foot-tall left field wall that has confounded heavy hitters for decades. The New England Patriots of the National Football League play in the Boston suburb of Foxboro.

The Trivia

Fact: Boston was a center of literary activity in the 1800s; many literary giants lived in the city, including Louisa May Alcott, Ralph Waldo Emerson, Nathaniel Hawthorne, and Henry Wadsworth Longfellow.

Fact: Boston Common is the oldest public park in the United States, covering 50 acres amid the city's downtown area. Until 1817 the Common was the site of public hangings.

Why Boston Is a *50 plus one* City

Boston is respected not only for its prominent place in American history, but also for its reputation as an exciting, livable city that emphasizes education, art and architecture. A visit to Beantown is a must for history buffs and those interested in the best of American culture.

11

Brussels, Belgium

The Basic Facts

Brussels is the capital of Belgium and the unofficial capital of the European Union. Over the past several years, the city's economy has grown substantially, so much so that the city struggles to preserve its historic treasures.

Geography

Brussels lies at 50 degrees 51 minutes north latitude and 4 degrees 21 minutes east longitude. The city is located in central Belgium and is the largest municipality of the Brussels-Capital Region. The city's population is estimated at only 140,000, but the metropolitan area's population is roughly two million.

Climate

Brussels has a temperate climate with warm summers and mild winters. Annual temperatures range from the lower 40s Fahrenheit in winter to the lower 70s Fahrenheit in summer. It can rain at any time of the year in Brussels, but snow is infrequent even in winter.

Government

The Brussels-Capital Region is divided into 19 regions or communes. Each commune elects representatives to the 89-member Regional Parliament in proportion to its population. The Parliament appoints regional administrators and approves the annual regional budget.

Demographics

Most residents are native-born Belgians or descended from the French. Brussels' population includes immigrants from other countries in Europe, the Middle East, and Africa. Dutch and French are the official languages of Brussels, although French is the usual language spoken by the people of Brussels.

Economy

Brussels is Belgium's center for the banking, insurance and transportation industries. Small industries manufacture ceramics, chemicals, drugs, processed foods, paper and textiles. The headquarters of several international organizations are located in Brussels including the European Union (EU) and the North Atlantic Treaty Organization (NATO); these organizations employ many local residents. Brussels is a hub for Europe's highway system and railroad network. City commuters use the Brussels Metro subway and an extensive tram and bus network. International travelers arrive at Brussels National Airport.

The History

The name Brussels comes from Old Dutch meaning marsh or home on the marsh, depending on the translation. In the late 10th century, Carl of France built a castrum (fortress) on an island in the Zenne. A new city wall was constructed in 1379, as the city had outgrown its original area (the wall is now known as the pentagon or inner ring). In the late 17th century Brussels was attacked by the French; more than 4,000 homes and medieval buildings destroyed by fire, but the famous city hall survived.

Brussels became the capital of Belgium when the first Belgian king, Léopold I, ascended to the throne in 1831. Brussels suffered greatly during both World Wars, especially in 1940 when the German army bombed the city relentlessly. Brussels gradually recovered in the post-war era, and its economy is thriving in the present day.

The Sights and Sounds

Brussels is a heart-shaped city divided into two sections. The Lower Section is the older part of the city and includes the Grand'Place (the main square of Brussels) and many historic buildings, some of which date to the 17th century. Most buildings in the Upper City, including the royal palace, parliament, and other government buildings are 100 to 200 years old. Around the Grand'Place are the Baroque guild houses, topped with golden statues and heroes which seem to have a life of their own. The Grand'Place is said to be one of the finest open spaces in Europe and has many cafes, shops and taverns, along with the popular Brewery Museum. The Town Hall also located here, is known for its statue of St. Michael crushing the devil; the building also displays a collection of historical tapestries, some of which date to the 16th century.

A must-see is the Grand Sablon, an expansive shopping and dining area with all its charm and sophistication. The Church of Notre Dame du Sablon and the Church of

Notre Dame de la Chapelle are among the finest Gothic churches in all of Northern Europe.

Many impressive museums beckon visitors, including the Fine Arts Museum with its collection of art by the Flemish and Dutch Old Masters. The Museum of Modern Art, in contrast, is as fascinating for its architecture as for the artworks displayed within. The museum is built eight stories into the ground around a natural light well. Music lovers will enjoy the Musical Instrument Museum, with some 7,000 instruments from as early as the Bronze Age. The saxophone, which was invented in Belgium, naturally has one of the larger displays.

Brussels' royal palace was rebuilt in the early 20th century to the specifications of King Léopold II, who was known for his expensive tastes. The palace has an especially grand stairway that leads to the throne room. Today the royal family does not live in the palace, but state affairs are frequently held there.

No one starves in Brussels, as the city has more than 3,000 restaurants and a host of cafés and eateries. Thirsty travelers can visit one of the many pubs for a draught of Belgium's renowned beers. Dance clubs open late and remain open into the wee hours of the morning. Brussels is an exciting city both day and night.

The Trivia

Fact: The Belgian Comic Strip Center is an entertaining museum dedicated to the fine art of cartooning.

Fact: The Belgian Constitution of 1971 attempted to quell the conflicts among French-speaking and Dutch-speaking Belgians. As a result, the country essentially divided itself in terms of linguistics; Brussels, however, remained bilingual.

Fact: Brussels is known as Bruxelles in French.

Why Brussels Is a *50 plus one* City

International visitors will be awed by Brussels' historical grandeur and contemporary vitality. It is a European city with a burgeoning economy and a growing global importance: truly a city on the move.

12

Budapest, Hungary

The Basic Facts

Budapest is the capital of Hungary and is a major center for politics, culture, transportation, and industry. It is among the most picturesque of Eastern European cities and is a popular tourist destination.

Geography

Budapest lies at 47 degrees 30 minutes north latitude and 19 degrees 5 minutes east longitude. The city is located along the banks of the Danube River in northern Hungary. Eight bridges span the Danube to connect the east and west sides of the city.

Climate

Budapest's climate is influenced by the Alps to the west and the Great Plain to the east. The city accordingly has humid, warm summers and short, cold winters. Average temperatures range from the mid-30s Fahrenheit in winter to the lower 80s Fahrenheit in summer. Rain occurs throughout the year.

Government

Budapest consists of 23 districts each with its own government, mayor, and council. The city government is headed by the city mayor, deputy mayors, chief clerk, and a 67-member general assembly. Twenty-eight departments within the mayor's office administer various municipal services.

Demographics

The majority of Budapest residents are native Hungarians. Most are Roman Catholic, although there are significant numbers of Calvinists and Lutherans. The official language is known as Magyar. The city's population is roughly 1.7 million.

Economy

Budapest was once a city of craftsmen who engaged in a variety of small industries, but World War II brought significant economic change to the city. Today large industries produce chemical products, textiles, transportation equipment, building materials, electrical equipment, and processed foods. Hungary's banking and finance industries are located in Budapest, as well as the primary hubs for the country's airlines, highways and railroads. Several ports along the Danube make Budapest an important trade center as well.

The History

The Romans built the town of Aquincum in the 1st century A.D. on the site of present-day Budapest. The invading Huns expelled the Romans in the 5th century. Over the next 4 centuries, the area was controlled by the Huns and other regional tribes. The Magyars, the ancestors of modern Hungarians, founded the Kingdom of Hungary in the early 11th century; the kingdom's realm eventually grew to encompass the cities of Buda, Pest, and Óbuda. Buda was home to the royal court and was an important city during the Italian Renaissance. Turks invaded the kingdom in the 16th century and retained control until they were ousted by the powerful Austrian Habsburgs. In the 19th century Pest became a center of Hungarian nationalism and culture.

Modern Budapest was formed in 1873 by uniting the three cities of the former kingdom. World War II was a particularly dark time for the city, as most of Budapest's Jews were eradicated by the Nazis. Hungarian Communists took control of the government after World War II, and the country fell under the influence of the Soviet Union. In the 1950s Hungarian freedom fighters revolted against Communist rule, and were brutally defeated in 1956 after Soviet troops marched on Budapest. Hungary regained its sovereignty following the dissolution of the Soviet Union in 1991.

The Sights and Sounds

The area known as Buda Castle was almost completely destroyed during World War II, and the area's original brilliance is slowly returning to the area by way of a lengthy reconstruction process. The Royal Palace is in this area of Budapest; this is not the original palace, although the museums located there today are built on its site.

The Ludwig Museum is the city's museum of international contemporary art, and the Hungarian National Gallery is devoted exclusively to the works of national artists. The Budapest History Museum displays information of the history of the city, from its liberation from the Turks in 1686 to the present day.

Matthias Church reflects the changing fortunes and religions of Budapest. The church was originally built in the 13th century as a mosque. The structure was destroyed and rebuilt in the 19th century, then destroyed again during World War II, and rebuilt once more. The church was the site of Habsburg coronations during their Hungarian rule.

Pest is the heart of the city, where visitors can see splendid examples of Budapest's history and architecture. The Hungarian State Opera House has been restored to its 19th century splendor; two marble sphinxes grace its entrance. The Hungarian National Museum opened in 1847 and is the home of the Hungarian Holy Crown and the coronation jewels. Its two permanent exhibitions span the whole of Hungarian history, and there is a contemporary exhibit that commemorates the end of Communism and the Russian troops' departure from Budapest.

The Great Synagogue, one of Europe's largest, was completed in 1859. Its grand organ is one of the finest of its kind and attracts classical musicians from around the world. Although the synagogue was virtually destroyed by the Nazis, restoration of the building is now complete.

The Parliament building stands along the Danube and is one of the most impressive landmarks of Budapest. The Holy Crown of St. Stephen, the country's first king, is prominently displayed in the building for all to appreciate. For a grand view of the city, ride to the top of the cupola at St. Stephen's Basilica, a massive 19th century neoclassical building. Heroes' Square and City Park offer a wealth of entertainment including a zoo, state circus, an amusement park, and mineral baths. Budapest has gained a fine reputation as a hotspot for dining and nightlife; many bars, cafés and restaurants have opened in recent years.

The Trivia

Fact: Buda is home to most of the city's historic churches and older homes. The Royal Palace (including the ruins of an ancient fort) dominates Castle Hill in the middle of the city.

Fact: Pest is the larger population center of the city and is built on a series of plateaus. Pest also includes the city's government offices and House of Parliament.

Why Budapest Is a *50 plus one* City

Despite centuries of war, religious persecution, and political strife, Budapest prospers today as a center of industry and culture in Eastern Europe. Increasing numbers of tourists flock to Budapest each year to delight in its historical treasures.

13

Buenos Aires, Argentina

The Basic Facts

Buenos Aires is the capital and largest city of Argentina, the country's main port and its industrial center. Nearly one-third of all Argentines live in Buenos Aires. Although Buenos Aires is considered one of the most beautiful and modern South American cities, it continues to struggle with housing and transportation problems.

Geography

Buenos Aires lies at 34 degrees 20 minutes south latitude and 58 degrees 30 minutes west longitude. The city is located along a broad, funnel-shaped bay called the Rio de la Plata in eastern Argentina, near the Atlantic Ocean. Buenos Aires itself is only 77 square miles in size, but the metropolitan area covers roughly 1,400 square miles.

Climate

Buenos Aires has a temperate climate that is influenced by the Atlantic Ocean. Annual temperatures range from the upper 50s Fahrenheit in winter to the upper 80s Fahrenheit in summer. Because Buenos Aires is located south of the equator, the winter and summer months are opposite from those in the northern hemisphere; winter occurs between June and August and summer occurs between December and February. Summers are quite warm and humid, making spring and fall the most pleasant seasons in which to visit. The city is rainy throughout the year, with the heaviest rains during the winter months.

Government

Buenos Aires is divided into administrative areas known as barrios (neighborhoods), based on the city's original Roman Catholic parishes. Each barrio has its own junta (city council) to handle local issues. The city government is administered by a mayor, appointed by the president of Argentina, and the city council, elected by the citizens. The scope of the city's municipal authority is limited by the country's government, located in the Buenos Aires federal district. By law, the president of Argentina controls the municipality of Buenos Aires and the National Congress enacts most legislation that governs the city.

Demographics

Residents of Buenos Aires primarily speak Spanish and are referred to as portenos (port dwellers). Nearly three-quarters of the city's population is of Spanish or Italian ancestry; other ethnic groups represented are French, German, Lebanese, Polish, Russian, and Syrians. The barrios are generally integrated, unlike other large world cities. The population of Buenos Aires is estimated at 2.9 million. Buenos Aires is a city of stark class distinctions. Elite upper-class families live either in suburban mansions or homes in the central city, while millions of lower-class families live in wooden shacks in the city's suburban slums.

Economy

Trade is the driving force in the economy of Buenos Aires; more than 80 percent of Argentina's foreign trade passes through the city's port. Agriculture, especially in the rich farmlands outside Buenos Aires, is also a vital component of the city's economic profile. Leading industries here include food processing, meat packing, and the manufacture of textiles, rubber products and electrical equipment.

Commuters to the city avoid traffic congestion by traveling on the oldest subway system in South America. Colectivos are another public transportation choice; these small buses carry some 20 passengers at a time. Ministro Pistarini International is the city's main airport; Aeroparque Jorge Newbery serves domestic air travelers.

The History

Buenos Aires was founded in 1536 by Pedro de Mendoza, the leader of a Spanish expedition on a quest for gold in the Americas. These settlers were repeatedly attacked by the indigenous peoples and escaped to Asunción, today the capital of Paraguay. In 1580 the Spanish conquistador Juan de Garay established a permanent settlement in Buenos Aires. In the 17th century the area was frequently raided by French, Portuguese and Danish settlers.

In 1776, the province separated from the Viceroy of Peru and became the capital of a new viceroyalty of the Rio de la Plata; this included much of present-day Argentina as well as Uruguay, Paraguay and Bolivia. During the Napoleonic Wars, settlers expelled British soldiers who occupied the province. This victory spurred an independence movement, and in 1810 an armed group succeeded in removing the viceroy and establishing their own provisional representative government.

Conflict raged in the ensuing years between those in favor of a strong central government and those in favor of local control. In 1880 the city was federalized and left the province, and La Plata became the new provisional capital. Railroad construction in the late 19th century brought tremendous economic growth and a large influx of immigrants. Shanty towns cropped up around the city, housing the burgeoning poor population unable to find jobs in local industries.

The dictator Juan Perón ascended to power in the 1950s, beginning an era of coups, brutal military dictatorships, and economic chaos. Tremendous inflation devastated the middle class and plunged the poor into greater poverty. The government initiated drastic economic reform in the 1980s when it aligned the Argentinean peso to the U.S. dollar, a move that had a significant negative impact on the local economy. Throngs of protesters poured into the streets of Buenos Aires as a succession of governments formed and fell in a matter of days.

The Sights and Sounds

There is a lively warmth and excitement in this very European city. Begin at the Museum of Modern Art of Buenos Aires; the collection includes works by both modern masters and emerging artists from Argentina and beyond. The National History Museum, housed in a family mansion, covers Argentina's history from the 16th through the 20th century. Artifacts from the 1810 War of Independence are prominently displayed, as are several paintings of battles during the 1870 War of Triple Alliances. La Boca Fine Arts Museum of Argentine Artists is a small facility, ideal for those interested in local art.

The Plaza de Mayo is a popular tourist attraction with a variety of sights and sounds: the National Bank of Argentina, a picturesque building with a vaulted dome; the Convent and Basilica of St. Francis, built in the 18th century and restored after being damaged during the Perón years; the Town Hall, an important site during the May revolution of 1810; and the Pink House, which houses the executive branch of government. The Metropolitan Cathedral, St. Ignatius of Loyola Parish Church, and St. Dominick Convent are dramatically beautiful examples of historic architecture.

The busy and pulsating area of el Centro gives Buenos Aires its reputation as a cosmopolitan city. Businesses, restaurants, and shops offer all sorts of entertainment for tourists. The nearby Military Circle, with its 220-foot-tall Obelisk, is a monument to Argentina's officer class.

The Colòn Theatre is among the world's finest opera houses, and has hosted every major opera star since it opened in 1908. Tours of the theatre are available, even if tickets to a performance are not. In the la Recoleta district, shopping, hotels, cafés and boutiques coexist in a delightful and comfortable area. La Recoleta Cemetery's 13 acres of above-ground vaults and crypts date to 1822. Two notable museums are nearby: the National Museum of Fine Arts, with some 11,000 works ranging from medieval to contemporary; and the National Museum of Decorative Art, which contains a vast collection of period furniture and art objects.

Nightlife in Buenos Aires does not even begin until 9 or 10 p.m., and clubs are open until the very wee hours. Buenos Aires is known as a café society in which locals frequently stop to enjoy coffee in a pleasant environment. The city has few skyscrapers, and so the many plazas, parks and broad avenues give the city an open, peaceful feel.

The Trivia

Fact: Eva Perón, one of history's more flamboyant characters, dominated Buenos Aires and Argentina politics as the wife of president Juan Perón. She died of cancer at an early age and became a beloved national icon. Her tomb is located at La Recoleta.

Fact: The name Buenos Aires is Spanish for fair winds. Early Spanish sailors named the broad harbor for Nuestra Senora Santa Maria del Buen Aire, the patron saint of fair winds.

Fact: In an attempt to curb traffic congestion, the city bans private vehicles from the downtown financial district during the day.

Why Buenos Aires Is a *50 plus one* City

Buenos Aires is a city of Argentines who think and act like Europeans. Life is easy here. The city is a rich blend of history and modern culture; truly a grand place to visit.

14

Cape Town, South Africa

The Basic Facts

Cape Town is the legislative capital of South Africa and has the country's third-largest population. After decades of international opposition and internal violence as a result of apartheid, the city has reinvented itself as a regional manufacturing center and popular tourist destination.

Geography

Cape Town lies at 33 degrees 48 minutes south latitude and 18 degrees 29 minutes east longitude. The city is located on the Cape Peninsula, also known as the Cape of Good Hope, and extends south from Table Mountain to the Atlantic Ocean. Cape Town is roughly 964 square miles in size. Surrounding communities that were segregated during apartheid have been merged into modern Cape Town.

Climate

Cape Town has a Mediterranean climate highlighted by warm, dry summers and cooler, rainy winters. Annual temperatures range from the mid-60s Fahrenheit in winter to the upper 70s Fahrenheit in summer. Because Cape Town is located south of the equator, the winter and summer months are opposite from those in the northern hemisphere; winter occurs between June and August and summer occurs between December and February. The Cape Doctor, a strong southeasterly wind, occurs frequently and is so named for its tendency to clear away air pollution.

Government

Cape Town is one of South Africa's six metropolitan municipalities and is divided into 105 municipal districts. Each district elects one representative to the city council. An additional 105 members are elected by a system of party-list proportional representation. The city council appoints the city mayor.

Demographics

Cape Town is a multicultural city including native Africans and European settlers. The majority of the population is Colored (of mixed African and European and Asian descent); other ethnic groups include Black Africans (most from the Xhosa tribe), Whites, and Asians. Cape Town residents primarily speak Afrikaans, Xhosa and English. The city's population is estimated at three million.

Economy

Historically Cape Town was the gateway to southern Africa, and today it is the second largest port in the country. Trade is a major part of the economy, and the city's harbor repairs, fuels and loads commercial shipping vessels. Goods manufactured in Cape Town include chemicals, clothing, processed foods, furniture, leather, automobiles and petroleum. Many Cape Town residents work in the thriving tourist industry.

The History

Abundant fossil and artifact evidence indicates that the Cape Peninsula was inhabited more than 600,000 years ago. The San were hunter-gatherers who settled in the area and relied on the sea for most of their food. Two thousand years ago, the Khoikhoi migrated from the north and displaced the San. The Khoikhoi, farmers and livestock owners, were the dominant tribe on the Cape until the mid-17th century.

The navigable Cape was a vital trade link that enabled ships to sail between the Atlantic and Indian Oceans. Vasco da Gama, a Portuguese explorer who reached India in 1497, was the first to round the Cape. In 1652 the Dutch arrived, under the command of Jan van Roebuck, and established a stopover on the Cape for their sailing ships. They soon constructed a fort at the base of Table Mountain; the settlement that grew around the fort became known as Cape Town.

By 1657, the Dutch East India Company allowed its employees to establish their own farms on the Cape; these people became known as Boers (farmers). The Khoikhoi and San populations gradually diminished, their people either killed by the settlers or by smallpox. Those that survived became servants of the Boers, who later aggressively took land from the Xhosa tribes. Their actions prompted a series of bloody wars that continued over the next century.

The Dutch relinquished the Cape to Britain after the Napoleonic Wars, and just as the Boers before them, the incoming British settlers took additional Xhosa land. The Boers chafed under British rule, and skirmishes between the two groups led to the Boer War between 1899 and 1902. Apartheid, the legal separation of whites and blacks, was a direct result of the Afrikaner nationalism movement of the early 20th century.

The Sights and Sounds

Cape Town blends old and new South Africa in a naturally beautiful environment unparalleled in a modern metropolis. Table Mountain looms over the city; those who reach the summit—either by cable car or by hiking its well-traveled paths—are rewarded with a spectacular view of the city and its environs. Cape Peninsula National Park is a short drive from Cape Town. This national treasure along the seashore contains a wide variety of South African flora and fauna. Hiking is a popular pastime in the park, but so too is sitting near the beach to watch the surf roll in.

Just seven miles offshore is Robben Island. The museum here was formerly the penitentiary where South Africa's political prisoners were held. Among its former inmates is Nelson Mandela, who was imprisoned here for 27 years and who later became the first democratically-elected president of South Africa. Tours are conducted by former prisoners, who are well-equipped to provide visitors with firsthand knowledge of the conditions in which they languished for many years.

The South African National Gallery is undergoing a renaissance, essentially rewriting the country's history to reflect the important contributions of Black Africans and other ethnic groups. The gallery prominently presents the works of South African artists, and describes itself as debunking cultural biases regarding attitudes and approaches to art.

Kirstenbosch Botanical Gardens always has something beautiful in bloom, for South Africa is home to some 9,000 native floral species. During the summer months, the Gardens host evening concerts. Groot Constantia Manor House is one of the oldest wineries in South Africa. Its Wine Museum serves to educate the public with social commentary and information on the lives of slaves who served there. The museum also includes a beautiful collection of furniture, textiles, and other objets d'art from the 19th and 20th centuries.

The Trivia

Fact: In 1867, fortune-seekers flocked to the area around present-day Kimberly after a rich diamond field was discovered on the site. The British quickly capitalized on the discovery, and in 1871 annexed the site as an addition to the Cape Colony.

Fact: In 1836, after years of resentment toward British rule, a group of Boers loaded their belongings onto ox carts and began heading inland, a historic journey that would come to be known as the Great Trek.

Why Cape Town Is a *50 plus one* City

Cape Town is a city of uncompromising physical beauty. It is also a city that lives with its past sins, unable to escape the realities of the bygone apartheid era and the ever-expanding AIDS epidemic in South Africa. But sorrow and shame give way to hope and a new future in this city dedicated to uniting all the peoples of South Africa.

15

Caracas, Venezuela

The Basic Facts

Caracas is the capital of Venezuela and is the country's largest city. Caracas was transformed in the oil boom of the 20th century as its population expanded and experienced greater social mobility.

Geography

Caracas lies at 10 degrees 30 minutes north latitude and 66 degrees 58 minutes west longitude. The city is located in a beautiful valley framed by the waters of the River Guaire and the coastal mountains, and lies close to the Caribbean Sea.

Climate

Caracas boasts a lush tropical climate that is consistently mild and spring-like throughout the year. Annual temperatures range from the upper 70s Fahrenheit in winter to the low 80s Fahrenheit in summer.

Government

Venezuela's executive, legislative, and judicial branches are all located within Caracas. The city is also the capital of the Distrito Federal (federal district); the district governor is appointed by the Venezuelan president. Caracas itself is governed by a democratically-elected mayor and city council.

Demographics

The multicultural population of Caracas reflects the population of the entire country. Caraquenians, as they are known, range from indigenous peoples to Western Europeans and Africans. The city has a well-defined class structure with a wide economic and cultural gap between rich and poor. Castilian Spanish is the official language of Caracas, but several indigenous languages are spoken as well. The population of the metropolitan area is estimated at 3.3 million.

Economy

Most Caraquenians work in the federal, provincial or local government; nearly 40 percent of Venezuela's government workforce lives in the city. The government-owned oil industry employs large numbers of residents. A small industrial base produces beer, cement, paper, and textiles. Caracas, like many rapidly growing cities, suffers from ongoing traffic congestion and air pollution. In an attempt to alleviate these problems, the city now has a modern subway system, the first section of which was opened in 1983. The city's airport, Maiquetia International, is located in the nearby suburb of Maiquetia.

The History

Caracas began as a Spanish settlement in 1567, when an expedition led by Diego de Losada discovered the beautiful valley and coastal range that framed the area. The indigenous peoples fiercely resisted the invaders, but Losada's landing party eventually defeated them. Losada publicly claimed the lands for the King of Spain, and in so doing founded the city of Caracas. In 1577 the city became the administrative seat of the Province of Venezuela; it was selected for its proximity to the sea, its rich land, and its ability to defend itself against pirate raids.

The city flourished over the next 200 years, but in 1812 was devastated by an earthquake. Some priests believed that the disaster was divine punishment for the citizens' growing revolt against Spanish rule. As a result, Simón Bolívar, himself a Caraquenian, led citizens in a successful attempt to reclaim Caracas for themselves. He became a hero in his native Venezuela, and earned the moniker el Libertador (the Liberator).

Caracas became one of the most prosperous Spanish colonial communities in South America, and grew steadily during the next 2 centuries. In the 1950s, Venezuelan dictator Marcos Peréz Jimenéz converted Caracas into a city with state-of-the-art, aesthetically pleasing buildings; funds for construction came from money raised during the oil boom.

The Sights and Sounds

Some may say that Caracas' improved cityscape has ruined this historic South American city. It has a functional, hurried style rather than charming and warm. Caracas lacks a central downtown, and as a result, the city's sights and sounds are scattered among various districts. El Centro is the oldest part of the city, where Caracas was originally founded. The Plaza Bolívar is a large open space in the city, surrounded by the best of old Caracas.

The National Capitol is a two-building compound founded on the site of a

17th century convent. The original buildings were dismantled in 1874 when religious orders were banned; new federal and legislative buildings were built on the site.

Casa Natal de Bolívar is the former home of el Liberador. Although the building is largely devoid of personal or historical memorabilia, it is nevertheless an excellent example of a colonial Venezuelan house.

Two churches in the area are worth noting. The Metropolitan Cathedral was built at the end of the 17th century and is home to the Bolívar family chapel. One of the best examples of colonial architecture in Caracas is the 16th century Church of San Francisco. It was the place where Bolívar declared Venezuela's independence; after his death his state funeral was held there.

The National Art Gallery has literally thousands of works of Venezuelan origin. The gallery shares space with the Museo de Bellas Artes, which has a broader international collection. Most major exhibits and cultural events are held at Bellas Artes. The Museum of Contemporary Art, with its extensive collection of modern works, is just off Central Park—which is not a park at all, but rather a concrete block of high-rise flats.

The night comes alive late in the evening—a problem for unsuspecting tourists in a city with a high crime rate. Follow the Caraquenians' example and do not venture into neighborhoods after dark unless you have a cab waiting.

The Trivia

Fact: The city of Caracas was originally named Santiago de León de Caracas: Santiago for the patron saint of Spain; León for the governor of the day; and Caracas in honor of the indigenous tribe that inhabited the coastal mountain range.

Fact: In the 19th century the Venezuelan ruler Antonio Guzmán Blanco was determined to transform Caracas into a South American version of Paris. He commissioned the construction of a series of buildings to reflect the designs of Parisian buildings.

Why Caracas Is a *50 plus one* City

Visitors to Caracas may view its class distinctions as being rather extreme, but the city is among the greatest in South America, and continually strives to take its proper place in history, art and architecture.

16

Chicago, United States

The Basics

Chicago is the third most populous city in the United States and the country's largest inland city. Among its many nicknames, the Windy City is the one best known throughout the world. Chicagoland is the name given to the city and its surrounding suburbs.

Geography

Chicago lies at 41 degrees 49 minutes north latitude and 87 degrees 37 minutes west longitude. It is located in the Midwest United States in the state of Illinois, where the Chicago River meets the southwestern shore of Lake Michigan. It is far and away the largest city in the Midwest.

Climate

Chicago is widely perceived to have bitter cold winters, although the average winter temperature is relatively mild for the Midwest. Annual temperatures range from the low 30s Fahrenheit in winter to the low 80s Fahrenheit in summer. Chicagoans are quick to mention, however, that the temperature can dip below zero in January and February and exceed 90 degrees in summer. As a rule, Lake Michigan has a moderating effect on temperatures in the city, making the lakeshore cooler in summer and warmer in winter; this phenomenon leads to the popular summertime expression, cooler by the lake.

Government

Chicago has a mayor-city council form of government. The mayor is the chief executive and is elected to a 4-year term. The city council is the legislative body and consists of 50 aldermen (currently, one-third of whom are women), one from each city ward. In the mid-20th century, corruption was rife among the ward bosses, giving rise to the expression, vote early, vote often.

Demographics

Chicago and its inner-ring suburbs have experienced a steady population decrease over the past 20 years as residents have sought more space in the outlying areas. The city's population is roughly 2.9 million, while that of the entire metropolitan area is 9.8 million. Chicago's population is the 14th largest in the world.

Economy

Chicagoland has a manufacturing base that is unparalleled in the United States; traditional manufacturing industries employ 15 percent of the total workforce. The area economy is now widely diversified, especially in financial services, education, publishing, and business services.

The History

The area around present-day Chicago has been inhabited by indigenous peoples for more than 5,000 years. The Potawatomi tribe is known to have lived in the area by the mid-17th century, for it was they who warmly welcomed the French-Canadian explorer Louis Jolliet and the French Jesuit priest Jacques Marquette as they canoed along the Chicago River.

In the 1770s, a Haitian fur trader named Jean Baptiste Point du Sable migrated from New Orleans to the Chicago area and established a trading post on the north bank of the Chicago River. A permanent settlement later formed on this site. In 1803, the United States built the first military post, Fort Dearborn, was built on the river's south bank. Illinois became a state in 1818 and granted a city charter to Chicago settlement in 1837.

Chicago became a major railroad hub in the Midwest, and stockyards were built to take advantage of the city's transportation potential. Chicago was also a prime lumber processing center at the time, and virtually all buildings in the entire city were constructed of wood. This is one reason that The Great Chicago Fire of 1871 was so devastating to the city. A small fire that began on the near south side quickly grew into a conflagration that raged through the helpless city for 2 days in October. The disaster burned 2,000 acres of property, wiped out well over $200 million worth of property, killed 300 people, and left some 100,000 others homeless. In the aftermath of the fire, city government enacted strict building codes in favor of masonry construction. Chicago reinvented itself in short order and became an architectural gem. Visitors to the 1893 World's Columbian Expedition stood in awe of the transformed city.

The decade of the 1920s was an infamous period in Chicago's history. Prohibition spurred the rise of several mob factions that warred with each other for control of the city's illicit liquor market. Riots followed the April 1968 assassination of Martin Luther King, Jr. and the Democratic National Convention that August. Chicago lived through these events to claim its place as a world-class city and center of architecture, culture and music.

The Sights and Sounds

Many visitors to the United States travel either to the East Coast or the West Coasts and overlook the Midwest. They therefore miss the opportunity to see Chicago, with its pristine lakefront, outstanding museums, and its lively culture.

The core structure of Chicago was built according to the Burnham Plan, named for the famous architect Daniel Burnham. Central to the Burnham Plan was the inclusion of green spaces and public areas: expansive lakeside parks, including Lincoln to the north and Grant to the south; free and accessible beaches; and marinas that hug the shoreline.

One of the best ways to learn about Chicago and its history is to take a river and lake tour. Architecture is what Chicago is all about, and the skyline is best seen from well out on Lake Michigan. Once the world's tallest office building, the Sears Tower is a definite must-see; ironically, Sears, Roebuck and Company, for which the building is named, moved its headquarters to the suburbs years ago.

Michigan Avenue is a fabulous upscale shopping area and a favorite with tourists. Nearby are the John Hancock Center, the historic Drake Hotel, and the former Palmolive Building, once home to Playboy Magazine. The Mies van der Rohe apartments hug the inner edge of Lake Shore Drive a short distance away. Go around the bend of the Drive to see the vintage condos overlooking Oak Street Beach.

The Art Institute is one of the finest multi-level museums in the world; but do not pass up the opportunity to see Chicago's many other gems: the Oriental Institute at the University of Chicago; the Museum of Contemporary Art; the Field Museum of Natural History; the Museum of Science and Industry; the Shedd Aquarium; Lincoln Park Zoo; and the wildly popular urban playgrounds Millennium Park and Navy Pier.

The Trivia

Fact: Chicago's nickname the Windy City does not refer to the weather–although the downtown area gets more than its share of blustery winds. A New York columnist coined the phrase when Chicago was competing rather loudly with New York for the 1893 World's Columbian Exposition.

Fact: The nuclear age began in Chicago when the first sustained nuclear chain reaction was accomplished at the University of Chicago on December 2, 1942.

Fact: The Chicago Water Tower, constructed of dolomite limestone, was one of the few buildings in the city to survive the Great Chicago Fire.

Fact: Chicago was the site of two deadly tragedies attributed to human error. The 1903 Iroquois Theater fire claimed more than 600 lives, and in 1915 the Eastland passenger ship capsized in the Chicago River, killing more than 800 people.

Fact: Chicago has also been called Hog Butcher to the World (after its enormous stockyards), Second City (until the 1980s it was second only to New York City in terms of its population), and The City of Big Shoulders (so named by the Illinois-born poet Carl Sandburg).

Fact: Chicago's motto is *Urbs in horto* (Latin for City in a Garden).

Why Chicago Is a *50 plus one* City

No American city has transformed itself over the last 50 years as much as Chicago. Once a gritty industrial town known for stockyards and steel, today's Chicago is a clean, sophisticated and artistic city. Chicago is the home of Encouragement Press, LLC.

17

Cologne, Germany

The Basic Facts

Cologne is Germany's oldest city and is the country's center of industry, commerce and culture. Cologne was devastated by Allied bombing during World War II; about 90 percent of the city center was destroyed, and the population decreased significantly due to the bombing and evacuation. But in Cologne fashion, the city bounced back strongly after the war. The city center was rebuilt, new infrastructure helped spur development, and Cologne's industries returned to full strength. The city has regained its status as one of Germany's most vital cities, and there is a rich and fascinating history to explore.

Geography

Cologne lies at 50 degrees 56 minutes north latitude and 6 degrees 57 minutes east longitude. The city is located in the German Federal State of North Rhine-Westphalia, in a larger region known as the Rhineland. Cologne covers about 156 square miles on both sides of the Rhine River. Industry is centered along the east bank and commercial and residential areas are located chiefly along the west bank.

The city's inner boundaries are delineated by the Ringstrassen, a network of semicircular roads that replaced the walls of the old city's medieval fortresses.

Climate

Cologne is within the North-West German lowlands and the climate is influenced by the Atlantic Ocean and the North Sea. Cologne has a mild climate with moderate precipitation, high humidity, and cloudy skies. Average temperatures range from the mid-40s Fahrenheit in the winter to the lower 70s in the summer.

Government

The city's administration is led by a lord mayor and two deputy mayors. The lord mayor and the 90-member city council are elected by the city residents.

Demographics

Cologne's residents are primarily German-born, and include Rhinelanders, Polish Germans (formerly Prussians) and German Turks. Many foreign immigrants come from Spain and Poland, and there is a large Japanese community in nearby Düsseldorf. The metropolitan area of Cologne includes more than 12 million inhabitants.

Many young people are drawn to Cologne due to its reputation as a permissive environment. Indeed, Cologne is one of only a few world cities where prostitution is legal; however, the city does charge an explicit tax on the industry.

Economy

Cologne, as well as the surrounding Rhineland, is a chief industrial center in Germany. The city's manufacturing industries include metals, automobiles, beers, chemicals, pharmaceuticals and petrochemicals. Electrical power generation is also an important industry here.

Cologne is an important river port and rail center, connecting the city to the rest of Europe. Germany's insurance businesses are largely headquartered in the city. Cologne is known for its famous *Eau de Cologne*, which is now manufactured in the city and elsewhere.

The History

Cologne began as a Roman settlement in 50 A.D. The Romans displaced the Ubil, an ancient Germanic people who had lived there for centuries. The Romans eventually established Christianity as the official religion of Cologne.

Charlemagne founded the Archbishopric of Cologne in 785; the archbishop became one of the most powerful figures in the Holy Roman Empire. The Middle Ages was a golden era for Cologne, unlike many cities in the area. At the time the largest city north of the Alps, Cologne was a member of the Hanseatic League and was more important commercially than the well-established commercial centers of London and Paris.

Cologne soon became one of the most populous in German-speaking Europe. The first municipal university in Europe was established there in 1338; and the city maintained its status as an economic and educational center for the next several hundred years. In 1475 Cologne officially became an Imperial Free City, meaning that the city was formerly responsible only to the Holy Roman Emperor.

Nineteenth-century industrialization was a boon for the city, which had quickly seized on the opportunities of new industries. Cologne's industrial output was hindered during World War I, but the city came back after the war. World War II, however, had a far greater negative effect on the city, as Nazi Germany engaged in widespread religious persecution. Four important synagogues were destroyed and many Jews were either imprisoned or murdered.

The Sights and Sounds

The Rhineland, including Cologne, is certainly one of the finest and most beautiful areas in all of Germany. As the Rhine meanders through the countryside, it passes vineyards, farming communities, and cities large and small.

Much of Cologne's early 1950s architecture and its associated blocky forms still exist today. However, the reconstruction following World War II yielded a significant change in the city's appearance. These architectural improvements have made Cologne one of the great cities of Germany and of Europe.

One of the reasons visitors flock to Cologne is to see the Old Town and its major attraction, the Cologne Cathedral (Kölner Dom), which is dedicated to St. Peter and the Virgin Mary. The cathedral was completed in the late 19th century, more than 600 years after construction began in 1248. Once completed, the Dom became the world's second-tallest Gothic structure. The cathedral's spires are a lofty 515 feet tall, and the height of its interior vault is nearly 139 feet. Like so many churches and cathedrals throughout the rest of Germany and Europe, the Cologne Cathedral was built to house relics of the Magi, who are said to have visited the baby Jesus. The 13th century gold and silver reliquary alone is worth a visit, as it is a glorious tribute to faith and church. Great nobles and bishops are buried within the cathedral.

The Germano-Roman Museum lies next to Cologne Cathedral. A fully-preserved mosaic floor was discovered on the site in 1941 as the government built an underground air-raid shelter to protect citizens from Allied bombers. Two other notable museums in Cologne are the Museum Ludwig, with its collection of 20th century artworks, and the Wallraf-Richartz Museum, which holds an extensive collection of art from the 13th through 19th centuries. Together, the three museums represent some 2,000 years of German and European art.

The Old Town Hall dates to Roman times as the center of Cologne's government and administration. Some of its statuary and embellishments are as much as 900 years old. One of the building's particularly interesting sites is a religious bath from the city's old Jewish quarter.

St. Martin's Square (Martinsviertel) surrounds the Great St. Martin's church, is a Romanesque treasure in an old section of the city that barely survived World War

II. During reconstruction, efforts were made to replicate the original medieval architecture. Schnutgen Museum, which houses a good deal of medieval art from the region, is a common tourist attraction.

The Trivia

Fact: Cologne was named by Agrippina, the wife of the Roman Emperor Claudius. Agrippina was born in the area and proclaimed the settlement Colonia. Agrippina was one of the most powerful women in Roman history and was the mother of the future emperor Nero. Interestingly, Nero ordered his own mother's murder soon after he gained power.

Fact: Roman influences are everywhere in Cologne. Remnants of the original city walls and first water pipes are evident. A section of the Roman road that connected Cologne to the Roman road network is now called the Hohe Strasse, and it is the most popular shopping district in the city.

Why Cologne Is a *50 plus one* City

Cologne is a fine city to visit. Travel the Rhine and take in the city's sights and sounds from various points of view. Cologne Cathedral alone is worth the trip. While many rave about the famous churches of Europe, it is certainly one of the most magnificent. The city is Germany at its best. Stroll and enjoy Cologne, a jewel of the Rhineland.

18

Copenhagen, Denmark

The Basic Facts

Copenhagen is the capital of Denmark and the nation's largest city. It is a major port and the center of Denmark's economy, politics and culture. Denmark is a constitutional democracy, and the royalty calls Copenhagen home. The city is a popular tourist attraction, as it is considered one of the world's major centers of culture and the arts.

Geography

Copenhagen lies at 55 degrees 43 minutes north latitude and 12 degrees 27 minutes east longitude. The city is located on both the eastern side of the Zealand, an island in the North Sea, and the nearby island of Amager. Copenhagen harbor, with its world-famous statue of The Little Mermaid (based on the story by Hans Christian Andersen), dominates the city. Town Hall Square forms the city center, and Copenhagen's main streets and highways extend out from the square.

Climate

Copenhagen's weather is mild throughout the year, with winter temperatures averaging in the upper 30s and summer temperatures averaging in the upper 60s. Rain and cloudy skies are common year round, but the climate is typically moderate.

Government

Copenhagen's local government is run by a committee system, as are most Danish municipalities. The government consists of a finance committee and six standing committees; each committee has its own area of responsibility and each is led by a separate adminstrator and mayor. The city's main political body is the City Council, which consists of 55 members who are elected for 4-year terms. The City Council directs the actions of the various committees.

Demographics

Copenhagen is divided into 15 city districts, and demographics vary among these areas. In general, Copenhagen residents are younger than those living elsewhere in Denmark. Native-born Danes comprise the vast majority of Copenhagen's population; however, immigration is on the rise from other European countries, primarily Scandinavia. The municipality of Copenhagen has some 500,000 residents, but the metropolitan area's population is more than twice this size.

Economy

As Copenhagen is Denmark's major port, international trade is a key source of employment for Copenhagen residents. The city is Denmark's industrial center and manufactures beer, diesel engines, furniture and porcelain. Like almost every major European city, tourism is a large part of the local economy. The city attracts many visitors each year, primarily from Europe and North America. Government services, in addition to industry, are a driving force of Copenhagen's economy.

The History

Copenhagen began as a small fishing village in the early 11th century. In 1167 a small fortress was constructed on the banks of the harbor to discourage raids by German tribes. The fortress was eventually destroyed by invaders, and Copenhagen Castle was constructed on the site.

Copenhagen became the capital of Denmark after 1416, when the reigning monarch King Eric of Pomerania moved into the Copenhagen Castle. In fact, during the 15th century Denmark also ruled Norway and Sweden, so at the time Copenhagen was the capital of three countries. Copenhagen grew rapidly in size and population over the next several centuries, but tragedy struck early in the 18th century. Bubonic plague would kill one-third of the population and two major fires would devastate the city's infrastructure.

During the Second Battle of Copenhagen in 1807, the British navy fiercely bombarded the city in an attempt to prevent the Danes from handing over its naval fleet to Napoléon. After Denmark became a democracy in 1849, the country experienced a period of relative peace and managed to maintain neutral status in World War I. During World War II, however, the Nazis occupied the city for 5 years.

The Sights and Sounds

Copenhagen is a city dominated by water; the presence of the sea and the various canals lends a maritime aura to the city. Although it is the largest city in Scandinavia—which includes Denmark, Sweden, Finland and Norway—Denmark's capital has a quaint, comfortable feel which invites visitors to walk the streets and bridges to see the sights.

Amalienborg Palace has been the home of the royal family since 1784. Tourists often visit the Amalienborg Museum within the palace, which presents a variety of royal family memorabilia as well as information about the history of Denmark and the art and artifacts of Copenhagen. A centerpiece of the exhibit is a formidable Viking ship.

The Botanical Garden certainly is one of the finest in Northern Europe, with special exhibits for tropical palms, orchids and cactus. In 1167 Bishop Absalon built the city's first walls and protection against raiders; in its place today is Christianborg Castle, built at the beginning of the 20th century as the Parliament House and Royal Reception Chambers.

There are many wonderful museums in Copenhagen. Of particular interest to visitors is the Hirschsprung Collection of art from the 19th century, Denmark's golden age. The Museum of Decorative Art has a large collection of handicrafts, silver and other artifacts from around the world. The National Museum, of course, contains the largest collection of art from all eras in Denmark's history, as well as fine displays of Egyptian, Greek and Roman artifacts and antiquities.

Do not miss the National Art Gallery, a 100-year old building that houses many 19th century Impressionist works. Also, the New Carlsberg Sculpture Museum displays a wonderful collection of Greek and Roman sculpture and art.

No one can visit Copenhagen without strolling through Tivoli Gardens, an amusement park dating from 1843. It is far more than the average amusement park! There are theatres, dance halls, beer gardens, rides, marching bands, upscale restaurants and concerts of all genres during the summer months. At night, the Chinese Pagoda, fountain and trees are illuminated with 100,000 white lights, and fireworks add to the festivities.

City Hall Square, dominated by the Town Hall building, is the business center of Copenhagen. The lookout at the top of the Town Hall's 350-foot-tower provides a marvelous bird's-eye view of Copenhagen. And the monument honoring Bishop Absalon, the city's founder, is prominently on display in Højbro Plads for all to admire.

If the view from the Town Hall is not good enough, try the top of the 600-foot Round Tower, originally built as an observatory in 1642 by Christian IV. There is an art museum halfway up the steps if you need a break from climbing! Also, you must include at least one church in your itinerary. The Church of Our Lady,

Copenhagen's main cathedral since 1924, is built upon the site of the original church that was completed in the late 16th century.

New Harbor is the center of Copenhagen's social scene. The area features restaurants, shops, bars and other attractions where one might enjoy a summer evening of drinking and fun. Old sailing ships in the harbor and delightful 18th century buildings provide a splendid backdrop for the area.

The Trivia

Fact: In the 19th century Copenhagen was a major center of culture. The philosopher Søren Kierkegaard, the theologian Nikolaj Grundtvig, and the artist Wilhelm Eckersberg (founder of the Danish School of Art) called Copenhagen home.

Fact: The writer most often associated with Copenhagen is Hans Christian Andersen. Andersen created some of the most beloved fairy tales of all time, and enjoyed great popularity in his lifetime and through to the present day. One of Copenhagen's most famous landmarks is The Little Mermaid statue in the city's harbor. The statue is based on a character from one of Andersen's stories.

Fact: Many of Copenhagen's most famous buildings were built during the Renaissance, including the Rundetarn (Round Tower), built as an observatory and still used for that purpose.

Fact: The Golden Age of Copenhagen in the late 1800s yielded great writers, architecture, and sculpture. Several grand neoclassical sculptures by artist Bertel Thorvaldsen were donated to the city during this time and survive to this day.

Fact: Many residents take advantage of the city's extensive system of bike paths and its bike-rental services. Not surprisingly, Copenhagen is sometimes referred to as the city of bicycles.

Why Copenhagen Is a *50 plus one* City

Copenhagen is a *50 plus one* City for its natural beauty, its rich history and the ease with which visitors can enjoy the city. Visitors flock to Copenhagen, if for no other reason than to see and enjoy the Tivoli Gardens–a place where greatness is displayed on a human scale.

19

Hong Kong, China

The Basic Facts

Hong Kong is one of the largest cities in the world. It is a Special Administrative Region (SAR) of China. China leased Hong Kong to the British in 1898, and under the terms of this lease, the city and region returned to Chinese control in 1997. China had declared that the relationship between the central government and the city would be one country, two systems. This led to the creation of the framework for Hong Kong's administration, known as the Basic Law. According to the law's provisions, Hong Kong retains its own executive, legislative and judicial systems. It remains a free port, issues its own currency and maintains its own police force. Defense and foreign policy matters remain under Chinese central government control. This arrangement has been largely successful to date, despite occasional protests by Hong Kong residents. Hong Kong has become a major world center for tourism.

Geography

Hong Kong lies at 21 degrees 45 minutes north latitude and 115 degrees east longitude. The city is located on the southern coast of China near the mouth of the Zhu Jiang (Pearl River). The city comprises a peninsula from the Chinese mainland and with 236 islands. The peninsula consists of the New Territories in the north and Kowloon to the south. Hong Kong Island, the main island, is south of the peninsula.

Hong Kong and Kowloon are the major cities in the Hong Kong SAR and are located on opposite sides of Victoria Harbour. Kowloon is the largest city, yet Hong Kong is the government seat and financial center. Tai Ping Shan (also known as Victoria Peak) towers over the city of Hong Kong, and various other mountains and rolling hills cover the region.

Climate

Hong Kong winters are cool and relatively dry with temperatures averaging in the mid-60s Fahrenheit. Summers are often warm and humid with average temperatures in the high 80s Fahrenheit.

Heavy rains typically occur in the summer and early fall, which lead to mudslides and flooding. As winters are dry, water shortages often result, and the city must then purchase water from nearby Chinese regions.

Government

Hong Kong's government follows the Basic Law. This system took effect on July 1, 1997 when control of Hong Kong was formally transferred from the British to the Chinese. The law established the one country, two systems policy, giving the Hong Kong region a high degree of autonomy. Even so, China's National People's Congress, which includes members elected from the SAR, must approve all Hong Kong laws.

The Hong Kong region is governed by a chief executive chosen by an 800-member election committee. The chief executive serves for 5 years, and committee members come from various socioeconomic classes and individual governmental bodies. The chief executive appoints members to an Executive Council, which performs the duties of the government. Hong Kong's principal legislative body is a 60-member Legislative Council. Hong Kong residents elect half of the council's members, and professional and special interest groups, called functional constituencies, elect the remainder.

Demographics

Almost all Hong Kong residents are native Chinese, including many immigrants from southern China. The non-Chinese minority consists of people from Australia, the United Kingdom, India, Japan, the United States and Vietnam. Over six million people live in the region.

Hong Kong's two official languages are Chinese (primarily Cantonese) and English, although most Hong Kong residents cannot speak or understand English. Urban areas are crowded, but recent settlements outside of the cities are attracting new residents. Small farming villages are responsible for the region's agriculture, which includes livestock and crops.

Economy

Hong Kong is an international center of trade, finance and tourism. It is a free port, meaning that there are no levies on incoming goods. Because of this, most goods sold in Hong Kong are inexpensive.

Most Hong Kong residents work in the service industry. A thriving industrial base generates textiles, clothing, electronics, plastics, watches and clocks.

The History

People have lived in Hong Kong for thousands of years. During the 1800s, British merchants openly smuggled opium into China and Hong Kong. Disputes between these merchants and the Chinese government led to the First Opium War (1839 to 1842). After the merchants prevailed, the Chinese ceded control of Hong Kong and surrounding area to Britain. In 1898 the Chinese leased the region to the British for a period of 99 years.

The population of Hong Kong grew quickly with a wave of immigration in the early 1900s. During this period, the Republic of China was born when nationalist revolutionaries overthrew the Manchu Dynasty. The Chinese Communists, who took control of China in 1949, never recognized Britain's control over Hong Kong, although they did not actively oppose British rule. Many Chinese fled Communist rule, and in the 1950s Hong Kong began to develop into a center of international trade, finance and industry.

The Sights and Sounds

Hong Kong is a bright, vibrant city with the soul of the East and the amenities of the West. You can find tailor-made suits, cheap electronics and fabulous food almost anywhere you look. The buildings are new, state-of-the-art and flashy. Hong Kong is also full of natural beauty, as it has a beautiful coast and has reclaimed much land by filling in coastal areas. Victoria Peak overlooks the city, and the rich and powerful live on the mountainside.

Victoria Peak is one of the key sights in the city. Locals suggest that first-time visitors ride the Peak Tramway to the summit, where the view is breathtaking. Most will tell you to go at night, so you can experience the grandeur of the illuminated buildings below. Every night at 8 p.m., Hong Kong's skyscrapers blossom with light in a show called the Symphony of Lights. A local radio station broadcasts music to accompany the show, and tourist attractions throughout the city carry this music as well. The different colors and types of light fascinate locals and foreigners alike.

The ferry route from Hong Kong to Kowloon offers unbelievable views of the area. Many experienced travelers to Hong Kong suggest that tourists ride the ferry twice during their visit. Go during the day to see the magical view of the water and coastline. Go again at night to see the skyscrapers lit up and to watch the light reflecting off the harbor.

In addition to the modern buildings and trendy houses, Hong Kong is also home to fascinating Chinese architecture, including various interesting temples that dot the city. Two of the most captivating temples are Man Mo Temple and Wong Tai Sin Temple; the buildings, statuary and incense that wafts through the air make a visit here well worth the trip.

Yuen Yuen Institute is an example of old-world Chinese architecture; its buildings are as beautiful inside as they are outside. The Institute is composed of monasteries and temples that represent Taoism, Confucianism and Buddhism.

In a city of imposing skyscrapers, the Bank of China Tower is in a class of its own. Designed by I. M. Pei, the 70-story structure is 1,209 feet tall and resembles a blue glass needle. There is an observation deck on the 43rd floor, which provides panoramic views of Hong Kong's skyline and coastline.

The Hong Kong Museum of History is the best place to learn more about the city. This museum is rather small considering Hong Kong's 6,000-year history; however, the museum has a fascinating exhibit on the history of the city.

The Hong Kong Museum of Art, with more than 12,000 pieces of Chinese art, houses one of the largest collections in China. For a small fee, you can view the museum's collections of calligraphy, silks, pottery and paintings.

The Hong Kong Space Museum is one of the largest planetariums in Asia. The museum opened in 1980 and features museum space as well as a theatre with engaging programs for planetarium visitors.

The Trivia

Fact: Hong Kong is both a region and a city, much like New York in the United States. Locals usually refer to the entire region as Hong Kong.

Fact: The name hong kong means fragrant harbor. The region surrounds Victoria Harbour, with Hong Kong on the northern part of Hong Kong Island and Kowloon on the southern part of the mainland.

Fact: The only time the population of Hong Kong decreased was during the Japanese occupation in World War II. The occupation was cruel and many Hong Kong residents fled to the relative safety of China–to return after the war.

Why Hong Kong Is a *50 plus one* City

No visitor to Asia can pass up Hong Kong: it is exotic, crowded, sophisticated and modern, all at the same time. It is difficult to imagine how this region grew from a small colony into the economic engine and cultural icon it is today. Hong Kong is a blend of East and West that is unmatched anywhere in the world.

20

Istanbul, Turkey

The Basic Facts

Istanbul has been one of the world's most important cities for centuries, serving at various times as the capital of the Roman, Byzantine and Ottoman Empires. Kemal Atatürk made Turkey a republic in 1923 and moved the capital from Istanbul to Ankara. Istanbul grew rapidly throughout the 20th century and the city underwent a series of civic improvements, including bridges across the Bosporus and slums and factories replaced with parks and playgrounds.

Geography

Istanbul lies at 41.02 north latitude and 29 degrees east longitude. The city is located at the south end of the Bosporus, a strait in northwestern Turkey that connects the Black Sea and the Sea of Marmara. Istanbul is unique in that it is the only metropolitan area on two continents, Europe and Asia.

Istanbul covers 769 square miles; the European side of the city is larger than the Asian side, and has a higher population. The European part of Istanbul is further divided by the Golden Horn, an inlet of the Bosporus; the northern section is more modern than the old section.

Climate

Istanbul's climate ranges from hot and humid in the summer to cold, rainy and even snowy in the winter. Temperatures average from the upper 40s in winter to the mid-80s in summer. Although summer is the driest season, there are usually no summer droughts, unlike other Mediterranean cities. The city is also quite windy with average winds of 11 mph.

Government

The mayor of Istanbul is appointed by the president of the republic, and is prefect of Istanbul city and governor of Istanbul il (province). The Emperor Constantine divided the city into 14 districts to emulate the divisions in Rome. Today, Istanbul is divided into 12 circumscriptions (kazas), each governed by a kaymakam.

Demographics

Muslim Turks comprise the vast majority of Istanbul's residents; Jews, Greeks and Armenian Christians largely constitute the city's minority. In the late 1960s, the population grew sharply, and by 1990 the population was roughly nine times what it had been in 1935. Half the city's residents are either native to Istanbul or from rural areas in Turkey. The metropolitan area's population numbers roughly 10 million.

Economy

Istanbul has been Turkey's cultural center for hundreds of years. City universities generate a good portion of the economy, but Istanbul's location also makes it a major trade center. It is also a major tourist attraction due to its rich variety of museums, mosques, Byzantine churches, palaces and bazaars.

Istanbul is the largest center of industry in Turkey. Its factories produce cement, drugs, electrical appliances, glassware, leather goods, machinery, plastics, processed foods, and automobiles and trucks. The shipyards on the Bosporus also maintain a lively business.

The History

The Asian part of Istanbul has been occupied perhaps as early as 3,000 years ago. In 667 B.C., Greek colonists founded the city of Byzantium on the site of what would become Istanbul. The city was absorbed into the Roman Empire, and in 330 A.D. the Roman emperor Constantine I declared Byzantium the imperial capital. After Constantine's death, the city was renamed Constantinople (literally, Constantine's city).

Sixty years later the Roman empire was split into two parts. Barbarians conquered the Western Roman Empire in the 5th century, while Constantinople remained the capital of the Eastern Roman or Byzantium Empire. Over the next several hundred years Constantinople would be attacked and conquered several more times. Ottoman forces conquered Constantinople in 1453, the city became the capital of the Ottoman Empire, and was renamed Istanbul. By the middle of the 16th century, following military campaigns into Europe and the Middle East, Istanbul had become a major center of politics, culture and commerce. After a period of decline in the 17th and 18th centuries, the sultans implemented various reforms to modernize the empire, including European style schools and other Western ideas.

The Ottoman Empire was defeated in World War I by the Allies, who occupied Istanbul from 1918 to 1923. In 1922 Kemal Atatürk, the father of modern Turkey, abolished the sultanate, made Turkey a republic, and moved the capital to Ankara.

The Sights and Sounds

The city of Istanbul is an amalgam of East and West, Christian and Muslim, Asian and European. There are two Istanbuls, in essence: Asian Istanbul, with Western housing and suburbs, and European Istanbul, the older and more historically significant area. The bridges that span the Golden Horn connect these two portions of the city.

The Old City is roughly the size of the original city as laid out by Constantine. It contains most of the city's treasures, including the Hagia Sophia, the Church of the Divine Wisdom, and is no longer a church or a mosque, but a museum. The original church was completed in 360, but the building and its successor were destroyed by fire. The current building was finished in 537 under Emperor Justinian I, and it remained the center of Eastern Rite Orthodoxy until it was converted into a mosque in 1453. In 1935 Kemal Atatürk established the Ayasofya Museum within the building. That Hagia Sophia survived at all is a miracle; neither earthquakes nor invaders destroyed the building or defaced its beauty.

While Hagia Sophia captures the city's history and culture, visitors frequently begin their tour of Istanbul at Topkapi Palace. Between the 15th and 19th centuries, the palace was the home of sultans and their harems. This important historical site includes such wonders as Hagia Eirene, the Court of the Janissaries (the royal guards), and the Gate of Salutation. Beautiful gardens and reflecting pools surround the palace's exterior. Remember to visit the harem, a popular attraction having nearly 400 rooms and apartments built around the sultan's quarters.

No visit to Istanbul would be complete without a visit to a bazaar. The largest of its kind in the city is the Grand Bazaar, a covered market with an estimated 4,000 shops and restaurants. The bazaar was built around 1450 and operates much the same as it has for hundreds of years. In addition, vendors at the nearby Egyptian (or Spice) Bazaar, built in the 17th century, sell a variety of foods from fruit to nuts.

The city of Istanbul contains some 1,000 mosques, and visitors favor two in particular. The Suleiman Mosque, named for the sultan Suleiman I, dates from the mid-16th century; this mosque is famous not only for its grandeur but also for the tombs of Suleiman I and his family. The Sultan Ahmed (or Blue) Mosque, is named for the sultan Ahmed I and is still a place of worship. This mosque, with its beautiful stained glass windows, was intentionally built opposite Hagia Sophia to rival the latter's architecture. Its original blue tiling gave the mosque its common Western name, although this tiling is now being replaced as inconsistent with the building's original appearance.

At one time, Istanbul had a stadium where horse races and other public events were held. The Hippodrome of Constantinople was a massive structure with seats for 100,000 spectators. Today only fragments of the Hippodrome remain, and the area has been converted into a square known as the Sultanahmet Meydani.

Yerebatan Sarayi (the Sunken Palace) is a cistern that dates to the 4th century during the reign of Constantine I. The Dolmabahçe Palace, so named for its surrounding gardens, is in the western part of the city and combines a variety of architectural styles and cultural aspects. Careful observers will note Hindu, Turkish and European influences on the building and its interior. The palace was built in 1853 as the residence of the last sultans of the Ottoman Empire. Notable features of this palace include the Crystal Staircase, decorated with Baccarat crystal, the 88-foot clock tower, and Kemal Atatürk's room in which he lived shortly before his death. Visit at night when the building is illuminated.

Nightlife in Istanbul is seemingly never-ending. At dawn, as devout Muslims face Mecca for morning prayers, revelers arrive to patronize the city's cafes, bars and nightclubs. The city also has a thriving theatre district.

The Trivia

Fact: At 3,000 years old, Istanbul is one of the oldest cities of the world and the only major city in the world that is situated on two continents.

Fact: Among the conquerors of Istanbul in the 12th and 13th Centuries were members of the 4th Crusade, who took the city in 1204. Crusader kings governed the city until 1261 when it was recaptured by the Byzantine armies.

Fact: Orthodox Christianity and Islam have had a tumultuous relationship in Istanbul, but for the most part the two religions coexist. The city has 25 Byzantine churches and more than 1,000 mosques.

Fact: Until 1930 the city was known colloquially as both Istanbul and Constantinople. In that year the Turkish government declared Istanbul the official name of the city.

Fact: Most of Istanbul's Greek population emigrated from the city in 1955 after the Istanbul Pogrom. Greeks now constitute a tiny minority of the city.

Why Istanbul Is a *50 plus one* City

Istanbul is the gateway to the Middle East and the geographic terminus of modern Europe. Straddling two worlds, it reflects myriad cultures, languages, customs and religions, all of which make this an exotic, culturally rich and entertaining city. The sights and sounds of this ancient city delight visitors.

21

Jakarta, Indonesia

The Basic Facts

Jakarta is Indonesia's capital and largest city, as well as the country's economic powerhouse. Following a period of violent political unrest in the late 20th century and attempts at government reform, unrest continues among rebels, students and terrorists both in Indonesia and Jakarta.

Geography

Jakarta lies at 6 degrees 17 minutes south latitude and 106 degrees 45 minutes east longitude. The city is located on the northwest coast of the Indonesian island of Java on the Ciliwung River. The city is mostly flat and dominates the island.

Climate

Jakarta is a tropical city featuring an annual rainfall of more than 67 inches and typical relative humidity between 75 percent and 85 percent. The climate is consistently warm; average annual temperatures range in the 80s Fahrenheit, although the high humidity often makes it feel much warmer. Because Jakarta is located south of the equator, the winter and summer months are opposite from those in the northern hemisphere; winter occurs between June and August and summer occurs between December and February.

Government

Jakarta is officially considered a province of Indonesia, not a city. Thus, a governor heads the provincial government. The province is divided into five city municipalities (kotamadaya), each headed by its own mayor (walikota) and regent (bupati).

Demographics

Jakarta is the economic and political capital of Indonesia, and as such the city attracts immigrants from the rest of Indonesia and from other countries. As a result, Jakarta has a rich culture and a cosmopolitan feel. Immigrants from other areas of Java speak a mixture of dialects of the Javanese and Sundanese languages, and they have brought traditional foods and customs to the city. The Orang Betawi Indonesian ethnic group is descended from residents of the surrounding area of Batavia, who came to the region to meet labor needs. These immigrants, with their distinct languages and culture, are rather different than the Jakarta Sundanese and Javanese. The city currently has more than 8.8 million residents.

Economy

The Indonesian economy is centered in Jakarta, and the Port of Tanjung Priok is the hub of much of the nation's foreign trade. Jakarta's factories manufacture motor vehicles, processed foods, chemicals, electronics, paper and printed material, and textiles.

The national and provincial government is a major employer, and employment in private industry has grown rapidly in recent years.

The History

The area around present-day Jakarta was settled by native peoples as early as the 5th century. Later, the area became part of the Hindu dynasty of Pajajaran, the last Hindu kingdom of West Java until the Portuguese arrived in 1522 to use the port for their burgeoning spice trade. The Muslim leader and Saint Sunan Gunungjati drove the Portuguese from the area, and renamed the city Jayakarta (victorious and prosperous).

The Europeans returned to the area in the early 17th century, when trade centers were established by Dutch and British merchants. Merchants battled for control of the region's trade, and the Dutch triumphed. The area became a Dutch colony, and would remain so until the Japanese invasion of Java in World War II.

After the war, nationalist leader Sukarno established the Republic of Indonesia, but the Dutch soon returned to take control of the area. A bloody civil war erupted in which nationalist Indonesians fought the Dutch and the British, who were aligned with the Dutch in support of trade in the region. Jakarta escaped most destruction during the war, although Sukarno briefly moved the capital from Jakarta to Yogyakarta to avoid Dutch repression. International pressure eventually forced the Dutch to withdraw, and in 1949 control of the country reverted to the nationalists. Sukarno declared martial law in 1957 and effectively became the nation's dictator.

Under Sukarno, Jakarta became a modern city and its infrastructure was much improved. Jakarta saw street combat in the 1960s as Sukarno battled his military leaders for control. After General Suharto seized power from Sukarno in 1967, the

Indonesian government was marred by corruption and nepotism. Suharto stepped down in 1998 after antigovernment riots claimed the lives of more than 500 people in Jakarta.

The Sights and Sounds

Jakarta is the largest city in Indonesia, and 60 percent of the population lives here. Amid skyscrapers, modern buildings and apartment houses, there are small houses made of bamboo and a fascinating local culture. The Indonesians are known for their shadow puppetry (Wayang), batik fabric and their orchestras known as gamelans.

National Monument (MONAS) celebrates the independence of Indonesia from the Dutch. It is 450 feet tall, with an observation deck that visitors can reach by elevator. The monument provides panoramic views of Jakarta and also contains an exhibit on the history of Indonesia.

The Jakarta Arts Center features live theater and dance programs; the gamelan, an Indonesia folk orchestra, often accompanies these events. Gamelans include a variety of metal and stringed instruments. The sound is interesting and uncommon to foreign visitors.

The Jakarta Museum in Fatahillah Square is housed in an ornate Dutch building from Jakarta's colonial period. It is a history museum with period furniture, arts and crafts, and significant information about Indonesia's Dutch colonial occupation.

Wayang Museum is dedicated to the shadow puppetry native to Indonesia. The puppets are flat and frequently made from buffalo hide. Performers move them against a screen that is illuminated from behind, so that the puppets look like shadows moving across the stage. Shows are based on folk tales and are often accompanied by music; shows are held most days. The museum also contains an impressive collection of puppets old and new.

Ragunan Zoo supports a wide variety of animals from Indonesia such as tapirs, komodo dragons and gibbons. The attached Schmutzer Primate Center is laid out so that the animals have room to move about in large enclosures. This state-of-the-art primate facility offers an opportunity to view gorillas and other primates in an area similar to their original habitat.

The National Museum includes thousands of artifacts from throughout Indonesia and Asia; its statues are particularly impressive. The galleries are large and clearly marked for tourists

Some of the most impressive orchids in the world are grown in Indonesia, and the many varieties are displayed at the Orchid Gardens. Many local greenhouses also allow visitors to view their flowers. The variety of colors and sizes of these exotic blooms is truly amazing.

The Trivia

Fact: Wealthy city residents once lived in a former Dutch section of Jakarta called Menteng; they now live in fashionable areas south of the city. Many Jakartans live in wood or bamboo structures called kampongs; sadly, these houses are typically found in slums with poor sanitation and a lack of potable water.

Fact: Chinese immigrants to Jakarta faced major repression in the 18th century. After troubles involving ethnic Chinese gangs, Dutch citizens searched many homes in immigrant areas and massacred 5,000 Chinese.

Fact: British forces allied with the Dutch launched a bloody attack in Jakarta on November 10, 1945. This day is now called Heroes Day and commemorates a galvanizing event in Indonesia's struggle for independence.

Fact: Like most densely populated cities, Jakarta suffers from significant air and noise pollution.

Why Jakarta Is a *50 plus one* City

A visit to Jakarta is a visit to the exotic East, where a melding of cultures has produced a fascinating and often complicated city. Teeming with people, it is a complex meld of old and new, East and West. The city has survived wars and political strife, yet still stands as a testament to the greatness of Indonesia.

22

Jerusalem, Israel

The Basic Facts

Jerusalem is the capital of Israel, one of the world's oldest cities, and the spiritual center of the Christian, Jewish and Muslim faiths. Britain took control of Jerusalem in World War I and administered it until 1947, when the United Nations voted to divide Palestine into Jewish and Arab states, with Jerusalem being an international city. This touched off violence and warfare between Jews and Palestinian Arabs that continues to this day.

Geography

Jerusalem lies at 31 degrees 46 minutes north latitude and 35 degrees 14 minutes east longitude. The city is located in the Judean Hills in Israel, about 40 miles east of the Mediterranean Sea, and consists of the Old City, West Jerusalem (also called the New City) and East Jerusalem. The West Bank, a highly disputed area inhabited by both Israelis and Palestinians, surrounds the city on three sides.

The Old City is the historical heart of Jerusalem and is enclosed by 40-foot stone walls. West Jerusalem is the most modern part of the city, and East Jerusalem is home to much of the city's Arab population.

Climate

Jerusalem is warm and dry, but winters can bring cold weather thanks to the city's altitude (roughly 2,500 feet). Temperatures average in the mid-50s Fahrenheit in winter and in the upper 80s Fahrenheit in summer. Jerusalem is rare among large world cities in that it has little air pollution.

Government

Jerusalem was deemed a single city under the Israeli government administration when East and West Jerusalem were united in 1967. The city is governed by a 31-member Municipal Council, elected to 5-year terms, and a mayor elected for a 4-year term.

Demographics

Jews comprise nearly three-quarters of Jerusalem's population, and Arabs primarily constitute the minority. Only about 50 percent of Jerusalem Jews were born in Israel; the remainder emigrated from Europe, the Middle East and northern Africa. Most Jews live in West Jerusalem, and most Palestinians live in East Jerusalem, although in recent years some Jews have moved into new East Jerusalem neighborhoods. Jerusalem's population numbers more than 700,000.

Economy

Tourism is the main driving force in Jerusalem's economy; visitors come to see the historic and religious sites that dominate the city's architecture. The population of Jerusalem boomed after Israel became independent in 1948, and construction has become an important part of the city's economy.

There is no heavy industry in Jerusalem, but there are small factories in West Jerusalem that manufacture chemicals, clothing, machinery, plastics, printing and foods. The city's many handicraft businesses produce pottery, glassware, silver, embroidery and carvings.

The city is accessible by highway and rail lines. Commuters typically travel by bus, and there are plans for constructing a light-rail system in the future. Ben Gurion International Airport, named for the first Prime Minister of Israel, is located southeast of nearby Tel Aviv and is the country's largest airport.

The History

Jerusalem has existed in various forms for more than 5,000 years. In about 1,000 B.C., David conquered the city and declared it the capital of the Kingdom of Israel. Later, after the death of King Solomon, tribal tensions led to the creation of two separate kingdoms: the northern kingdom of Israel and the southern kingdom called Judah. Jerusalem remained the capital of Judah.

Throughout the centuries, Judah was invaded and conquered by Babylon, Persia and Alexander the Great. In 63 B.C. the kingdom of Judah became a client-kingdom of the Roman Empire and was renamed Judea. Rome maintained control of the area for more than 100 years, but in 66 A.D. a group known as the Zealots revolted against Roman rule and seized Judah and Jerusalem. Four years later the Romans, under Titus, destroyed most of the city. Jerusalem remained uninhabited until 130, when the Romans rebuilt the city and constructed temples to Roman gods.

Christianity became the official religion of the Roman Empire in 325, and under Emperor Constantine these temples were replaced by Christian churches. Muslim

Arabs took control of Jerusalem in 638 and held it until 1099, when the First Crusaders conquered the city and decimated its Muslim population. In 1517, the Ottoman Empire conquered Jerusalem; it would remain under Ottoman control for 400 years.

Jews returned to the city during this period, and by 1870 constituted the majority population. Britain took control of Jerusalem during World War I and administered it until 1947, when the 1947 UN Partition Plan divided Israeli territory into Jewish and Arab states.

The Sights and Sounds

Jerusalem is one of the oldest cities in the world, and you cannot walk the narrow cobbled streets of the Old City without imagining the scene during biblical times. The rest of Jerusalem, however, is modern and utilitarian. In some areas, ancient and modern structures lie next to one another on the same street. The city's main industry is tourism, and tourists from all over the world flock to the holy sites of Islam, Christianity and Judaism.

The Old City is roughly a third of a mile square and perfect for walking. In fact, the narrow streets make most automobile travel impossible. The Old City Gates are of particular interest, as well as the area's four major neighborhoods: Muslim, Jewish, Christian and Armenian.

The Western Wall, also called the Wailing Wall, it is the only surviving section of the Second Temple. The wall is a holy place for Jews, who visit the wall to mourn the loss of their sacred shrine. The Church of the Holy Sepulchre is regarded by biblical scholars as the site of Golgotha, where Jesus is believed to have been crucified.

The Temple Mount is an area of the Old City sacred both to Jews and Muslims. Jews believe that ancient temples were built here, and Muslims believe that Muhammad ascended to heaven at the site of the Dome of the Rock.

The Mount of Olives is believed to be the site at which Jesus last saw his disciples before ascending to heaven. Another common pilgrimage site is the Via Dolorosa, a street in the Old City through which Jesus is thought to have carried the cross. The Via Dolorosa ends at Golgotha (the Place of the Skull, or Calvary), where Jesus is said to have been crucified.

While in Jerusalem, many tourists visit Yad Vashem, Israel's memorial to the victims of the Holocaust and the largest museum of its kind in the world. The Citadel (Tower of David) Museum is something of a misnomer. This site is believed to be a former palace of King David, but this is probably not the case. Nevertheless, the museum contains an extensive collection detailing the history of Jerusalem.

The Garden of Gethsemane is the site where biblical scholars believe Jesus was betrayed by Judas. There is a church here, as well as olive trees that date back thousands of years.

The Trivia

Fact: Jerusalem is a holy city Jews, Christians and Muslims. These groups, especially the Jews and Muslims, have vied for control of the Temple Mount and continue to do so.

Fact: Jerusalem is a union of several ancient cities: the Old City, which occupies most of Biblical Jerusalem; West Jerusalem, which is the most modern part of the city; and East Jerusalem, where most of Jerusalem's Arabs reside.

Fact: According to tradition the Prophet Muhammad selected Jerusalem as the qibla, towards which the Muslims should face during prayer. Muhammad later declared Mecca the focus of prayer so as to symbolize the independence of Islam.

Fact: Jewish immigration to Jerusalem increased rapidly in the 1920s and 1930s, fueled both by Nazi persecution in Europe and by a growing Zionist movement that aimed to create a Jewish homeland in Palestine. It was during this time that many Jewish neighborhoods were established, primarily in West Jerusalem.

Why Jerusalem Is a *50 plus one* City

If there is any city that is complicated by history, politics and religion, it is Jerusalem. That said, this is the very reason why the city is one of the greatest in the world. Although other large cities have more modern, sophisticated sights and sounds, people visit Jerusalem for the rich cultural and religious heritage that is its lifeblood.

23

Johannesburg, South Africa

The Basic Facts

Johannesburg is the largest city in South Africa and the capital Gauteng Province. Some of the earliest human fossils were discovered in this region. Following the demise of the apartheid government in 1994, Johannesburg has been moving toward a new era of racial tolerance.

Geography

Johannesburg lies at 26 degrees 8 minutes south latitude and 27 degrees 54 minutes east longitude. The city is located in Gauteng Province in northeastern South Africa. Johannesburg lies within the Witwatersrand, a 60-mile-long mountain range that runs through Gauteng. The Johannesburg metropolitan area includes the communities of Midrand, Randburg, Roodepoort, Sandton, Alexandra, Ennerdale, Lenasia and Soweto.

Climate

Johannesburg lies roughly 5,700 feet above sea level. The climate is sunny, mild and dry. Annual temperatures range from the mid-60s Fahrenheit in winter to the upper 70s Fahrenheit during the summer. Note that because South Africa lies south of the equator, the winter and summer months are opposite from those in the northern hemisphere. Thus, winter occurs between June and August and summer occurs between December and February.

Government

Johannesburg's first post-apartheid City Council, established in 1995, subdivided the city into four regions. Each region's authorities have substantial autonomous authority, yet the City Council is governed by a central metropolitan council.

Johannesburg's financial situation had fallen into disarray by 1999; in that year a city manager was appointed to reorganize the city's finances. This manager, together with the Municipal Council, coordinated plans for Igoli 2002, a blueprint to bring Johannesburg out of insolvency and into financial surplus.

Demographics

Black Africans are the majority group in Johannesburg, comprising 73 percent of the population; Caucasians, Colored South Africans (i.e., mixed racial) and Asians make up the remainder. Residents primarily speak Nguni or Sotho; one-quarter speak either English or Afrikaans (a derivation of Dutch). More than 3.2 million residents live in Johannesburg.

Economy

Johannesburg is South Africa's financial hub and the country's economic center. Although gold mining was once the city's main industry, the mines are no longer in operation. Even so, the headquarters of many mining companies are still located here. Gold, uranium, silver and diamonds remain an important part of Johannesburg's economy; however; other industries include steel and cement manufacturing.

Despite the city's economic advances, nearly 40 percent of Johannesburg's residents are chronically unemployed.

The History

In the 1820s the Ndebele leader Mzilikazi invaded the region surrounding Johannesburg. Mzilikazi was defeated in 1837, allowing Boers (white farmers from the Cape region) to establish settlements in the region.

After the Boer War of 1880, the British, who had annexed the Transvaal, allowed the settlers more independence. The region's fortunes changed dramatically in 1886, when one of the world's largest gold deposits was discovered on the Witwatersrand. Johannesburg was founded that year as a result of the gold rush and became a free-wheeling mining town. The city was named after Johann Rissik, the city's first surveyor-general, and Christiaan Johannes Joubert, the original vice president of the Transvaal republic.

An influx of enterprising foreigners and nearby black laborers caused the area's population to grow rapidly after the discovery of the Witwatersrand gold deposit. Over time Johannesburg evolved into a center of commerce and government.

Apartheid, South Africa's legalized form of segregation, was established in 1948 and continued into the early 1990s. Johannesburg became the flashpoint for resistance among Black and Colored Africans, who rebelled against the disparity inherent in the system. Many countries throughout the world also objected to apartheid and imposed economic sanctions on South Africa.

Johannesburg continued to thrive, but change was inevitable, especially after the 1990 release of anti-apartheid activist Nelson Mandela from prison. Mandela became the first president of South Africa after the abolition of apartheid in 1994. Since that time, South Africa's economy and international reputation have significantly improved.

The Sights and Sounds

Johannesburg is a modern city with a long history. Now that the specter of apartheid is behind it, the city is set for new growth and endless potential. Tourists come to Johannesburg to see its host of museums, art galleries, clubs, restaurants and nightlife.

The Apartheid Museum offers a multimedia glimpse into the city's apartheid era. This museum, which opened in 2001, contains a number of audio and video exhibits created by a series of South African filmmakers, historians and designers.

Visit the Origins Centre for a fascinating history of humanity as well as an exhibit on genetic testing and ancestral research. The collection houses excellent examples of early human skeletons; you can also visit the archeological digs currently underway in South Africa.

The Mandela Family Museum is located in Soweto, a poor neighboring township of Johannesburg. The modest former home of Nelson Mandela, the museum's collection tells the story of Mandela's life and imprisonment, as well as the history of apartheid.

Constitution Hill is a former prison containing multimedia exhibits describing the treatment of once-incarcerated criminals. The museum is one of Johannesburg's newest historical landmarks and is near the city courts, where visitors may watch trials and other court proceedings.

Johannesburg Art Gallery is the largest of its kind in sub-Saharan Africa. The collection not only includes South African works of art, but also those of international artists such as Picasso, Monet and Degas. The three-story building has 15 exhibit halls and sculpture gardens in adjoining Joubert Park.

AECI Dynamite Factory Museum exhibits the history of explosives used in Johannesburg's mining industry. Mining companies use dynamite to penetrate the rock that covered the rich diamond lodes in the Johannesburg area.

A trip to South Africa would be incomplete without a trip to one of the wild game reserves that surround the city. Visitors can hike and picnic in certain areas, and can ride trucks through the park. Common sights include gazelles, lions, hippos and wild dogs.

Johannesburg's current mining operations center on diamond extraction; however, the natural resource originally mined here was gold. Gold Reef City is a theme park with exhibits on the discovery, mining, and use of this important metallic element. The park recreates Johannesburg as it looked when gold was discovered there.

Soweto–a name derived from South Western Townships–is the site of primarily Black African ghettos near Johannesburg. Residents of these townships engaged in uprisings that eventually led to the demise of apartheid. Experts strongly recommend that visitors to this area take guided tours.

Erikson's Diamond Centre houses exhibits on the art of diamond cutting, as well as shops where visitors may purchase diamonds and have them made into jewelry.

The Trivia

Fact: South Africa recognizes 11 official languages. Most Johannesburg locals do speak English, but they have their own idiomatic expressions that may perplex tourists.

Fact: There are more than six million trees in the metropolitan area of Johannesburg. The summer and winter months are reversed due to South Africa's location south of the equator. Although the area is usually dry, frequent rainstorms occur in summer; visitors are advised to bring raingear.

Fact: Guateng, the province in which Johannesburg lies, literally means Place of Gold. Guateng is an apt name for this area in which a significant gold deposit was discovered in the 19th century.

Fact: The Johannesburg Fort, built shortly after the city's founding in 1886, was constructed not as a defense against invaders, but as a means to control the area's early mining population. The fort became a prison after the Anglo-Boer War of 1899 to 1902. The prison is now closed, and the site is being converted into the new home of South Africa's Constitutional Court.

Fact: Johannesburg's boundaries expanded after apartheid to include surrounding communities of poor Black Africans under the old system these areas were separately administered. The city's current boundaries were finalized in 2000.

Fact: South Africa is the largest diamond producer in the world and is the home of the DeBeers diamond empire.

Why Johannesburg Is a *50 plus one* City

Despite a troubled past, Johannesburg is a city of multiple cultures. European and African cultures now exist side by side, and that fact alone has made Johannesburg a city with great cultural importance.

24

Las Vegas, United States

The Basic Facts

Las Vegas is famously known as Sin City; gambling, resorts, shows and other activities have given the city an anything goes reputation. It is also fast becoming a popular convention center. The city lost some of its luster in the 1970s and early 1980s, but was reborn in the 1990s as luxurious mega-resorts were constructed and the city recast itself as a family tourist center. The city's current rapid growth contributes to problems such as high water usage, crowded schools and urban sprawl. Most visitors, however, are not aware of these problems as they crowd the Las Vegas casinos, showplaces and wedding chapels.

Geography

Las Vegas lies at 36 degrees 12 minutes north latitude and 115 degrees 10 minutes west longitude. This was a grassland area when the city was incorporated in 1911– its name is derived from vegas, or meadows in Spanish–although it is in now in the midst of the Mojave Desert.

Las Vegas is the county seat of Clark County, and the metropolitan area includes Nye County in Nevada and Mohave County in Arizona. Nearly half of the urban area referred to as Las Vegas (including Fremont Street and the Las Vegas Strip) lie outside the actual city limits.

Climate

For most of the year, Las Vegas has a warm and dry climate; any significant rainfall occurs in the winter months. Winter temperatures average in the lower 60s Fahrenheit, but summer temperatures often exceed 100 degrees Fahrenheit. Many say that it is not the heat; it is the humidity. Indeed, Las Vegas' low humidity makes the brutally hot summers somewhat more bearable than less arid portions of the country.

Government

Las Vegas is run by a city council and city manager. The mayor and six council members are elected to 6-year terms and appoint a city manager to administer policies and city operations. Clark County is governed by seven commissioners who are elected to 4-year terms, and they appoint a county manager with similar administrative duties.

Demographics

Nearly 70 percent of Las Vegas residents are Caucasian; the remainder are African-Americans, Latinos, Native Americans and Asians. The city has more than 500,000 residents, although the population has been growing rapidly since the mid-1990s.

Most Las Vegas residents are not native to the area, but come from throughout the country and around the world. The city's recent economic boom is responsible for its significant population growth.

Economy

Las Vegas' economy is driven primarily by tourism and conventions. The Las Vegas Convention Center is the largest single-level convention center in the United States, and more than three million people attend conventions in Las Vegas every year.

While most Las Vegas residents are employed in the service industry, the federal government is also a major employer. Nellis Air Force Base and Range are located nearby, and the Nevada Test Site is located 65 miles northwest of the city.

The History

In 1855 Mormons settled the surrounding area to serve as a stopover for travelers between Salt Lake City and San Bernardino. The city was established in 1905, when the San Pedro, Los Angeles and Salt Lake Railroad company auctioned off its lands. The town's population grew to 1,000 in 1910, and was incorporated as a city in 1911. Nevada legalized gambling in 1931, but in 1935 construction began on a federal project that would transform the region. Hoover Dam, a 726-foot-high concrete arch-gravity dam on the Colorado River, was built over 5 years by more than 21,000 workers. These workers flocked to Las Vegas in their off hours and money began to pour in to the city's coffers. The Flamingo Hotel, the first large casino, opened in 1946 and a steady succession of others followed.

Fremont Street and the Strip became the city's two major recreational areas. The city developed rapidly during the 1950s and 1960s and organized crime held sway over many of the casino hotels. Today, Las Vegas is a tourist mecca and has recreated itself—for the most part—as a family-oriented attraction.

The Sights and Sounds

The sights and sounds of Las Vegas cannot be described in a few words. Unlike other world cities, the history, architecture and fine arts do not attract visitors; tourists come for fun, gambling, live shows, dining, and just about every other possible recreation. There is something for everyone in Las Vegas.

Although Las Vegas is a relatively small city, distances are deceptive on Fremont Street and the Strip because the hotels and casinos are simply enormous. A stroll to the next building often takes 10 or 15 minutes. The Strip is more popular than the downtown area, but several points of interest continue to attract visitors to the latter. The most famous of these is the Fremont Street Experience, a pedestrian mall that is enclosed by a huge awning illuminated by millions of lights. The Experience is said to be the most brightly-lit area in the world. Another attraction is the Viva Vision, a 90-foot-tall video display–the largest in the world–that screens state-of-the art audiovisual shows nightly. The Viva Vision cost $17 million to build, and its nightly operating cost must be immeasurable.

One of the classic casinos downtown is the Golden Nugget, named for the 60-pound gold nugget on display in the hotel lobby. The property opened in 1946 and is currently undergoing renovations to attract visitors otherwise drawn to the Strip.

Only Las Vegas would house the Neon Museum, whose mission is to preserve and display neon signs from the 1940s to the present. The museum runs an outdoor walking tour of some of its pieces that have been restored as public art. The Museum opened its doors in 1996 when the world-famous Hacienda Horse and Rider sign was installed at the corner of Fremont Street Experience and Las Vegas Boulevard.

The Stratosphere Tower, at 1,149 feet, is the tallest building west of the Mississippi River. Visitors can get a terrific view of the surrounding area from the tower's observation deck. The Top of the World restaurant, 800 feet up, revolves in a complete circle in 80 minutes. The tower's three thrill rides, however, are the main attraction. These rides, at the very top of the tower, are definitely not for the faint of heart.

Nothing says Las Vegas more than the four-mile stretch of Las Vegas Boulevard known as the Strip. This remarkable area regularly reinvents itself to change with the times. Casino Hotels are razed and rebuilt when they are no longer large enough, fancy enough, or popular enough to appeal to visitors. Among the best-known properties are:

- Bellagio–the second largest casino in Las Vegas;
- Caesar's Palace–an opulent Roman-themed casino;

- Circus Circus–a vintage casino hotel with a circus motif;
- Flamingo–built in 1946 by the infamous gangster Bugsy Siegel;
- Luxor–with visions of ancient Egypt;
- MGM Grand–a property with a Hollywood flavor;
- Mirage–with a South Seas atmosphere; and
- Tropicana–a lush, tropical oasis with a popular swimming pool.

No visit to the city is complete without a side trip to Hoover Dam and Lake Mead. The Hoover Dam tamed the Colorado River to harvest hydro-electric power. The dam's construction resulted in Lake Mead, the largest man-made lake in the western hemisphere and a playground for boaters, fishing enthusiasts and swimmers from around the world.

The Trivia

Fact: Ironically, the area that became Sin City was originally settled by Mormons.

Fact: The wealthy eccentric Howard Hughes came to Las Vegas in 1966 and purchased several casino hotels; transactions that effectively ended mob control over the area. While living in Las Vegas, Hughes was a recluse who never left his residence on the ninth floor of the Desert Inn.

Fact: The city's economy is partly driven by the United States government. Before the Nuclear Test Ban Treaty was implemented, Las Vegas residents would regularly see mushroom clouds rise from the desert.

Fact: There are no clocks in casinos, an intentional decision designed to encourage gamblers and other patrons to stay and spend their money.

Why Las Vegas Is a *50 plus one* City

Las Vegas is a modern marvel, exuding excess like no other place in the world. The city is fun and entertaining: the sinful capital of the world. Most everyone wants to visit Las Vegas at least once, and for good reason.

25

Lima, Peru

The Basic Facts

Lima is the capital and largest city of Peru, and the country's center for commerce, industry and culture. The city grew in a chaotic fashion during the 20th century, due to an influx of rural Peruvians. Lima's architecture blends 16th century mansions with modern buildings in its business district. There is a rigid class structure in Lima based on race and ethnicity, but for the visitor Lima is a striking example of one of South America's first capital cities.

Geography

Lima lies at 12 degrees 6 minutes south latitude and 76 degrees 55 minutes west longitude. The city is located in west-central Peru, less than 10 miles from the Pacific Ocean, in the lowlands to the west of the Andes Mountains.

Climate

Lima's climate is relatively moderate due to its proximity to the Andes Mountains and the Pacific Ocean. The cold Humboldt current helps add to the ocean's moderating effects. Average temperatures range from the upper 60s Fahrenheit in winter to the lower 80s in summer. Because Lima is located south of the equator, the winter and summer months are opposite from those in the northern hemisphere; winter occurs between June and August and summer occurs between December and February. The climate can also be rather humid, and Lima is prone to heavy fogs from May through November.

Government

The Peruvian government is comprised of 12 regions and 24 departments, which are subdivided into provinces and districts within provinces. Lima, a province in itself, has 30 districts. A mayor and the Metropolitan Lima Municipal Council have authority over the city's districts.

Demographics

As one of South America's largest cities, Lima is ethnically diverse. Mestizos, those of mixed Spanish and American Indian descent, historically dominated the Lima population. In the late 20th century, however, political and economic instability spurred the immigration of Campesinos (full-blooded American Indians) from the Andean highlands. The Campesinos, most of whom live in poverty-stricken shantytowns, speak native languages of Quechua and Aymara.

Lima's population also includes residents with Spanish, Italian, German, and African ancestry (Afro-Peruvians are descendants of Africans brought to Peru by the Conquistadors). Interestingly, Lima has one of South America's largest concentrations of Japanese and Chinese immigrants.

Economy

Lima's economy is primarily national government-based. Lima is also Peru's manufacturing center, with industries producing textiles, paper, paint and food products. Retail business has grown rapidly in the past 2 decades and shopping malls have sprung up throughout the city. Museums and cultural features also attract significant numbers of tourists, which contributes to economic growth.

The History

The earliest residents of Peru were likely North American Indians who migrated to the area approximately 12,000 years ago. Lima is built on an area where civilizations built monuments and settlements as early as 2800 B.C. Between 1100 and 1300 A.D., the Incas founded a kingdom in Peru; Incans were skilled architects and builders, and they created many of Peru's greatest historical treasures.

By the early 1500s, before the Spanish Conquistadors arrived, the Incan empire that included the present-day countries of Peru, Colombia, Ecuador, Chile and Argentina. In 1532 a Spanish expedition led by Francisco Pizaro arrived in Peru seeking purported treasures of silver and gold. Pizarro remained in the region and founded Ciudad de los Reyes in 1535 on the site of what would become Lima.

During the Spanish Colonial era, viceroys from the Hapsburg court in Spain ruled the country. In the early 1800s Peruvians rebelled against Spanish control with the help of armed forces from neighboring countries. The rebels were successful, and in 1821 Peru became an independent nation. Lima would witness several skirmishes for power in the next few decades, along with a succession of governments, but the city continued to flourish. Lima was sacked during a lengthy war with Chile and Bolivia that began in 1879. Post-war reconstruction essentially transformed Lima into a new city.

The Sights and Sounds

Visitors can explore a good deal of historical and colonial Lima by focusing on the city center around the Plaza Mayor, an enormous 16th century square. The museums are not centrally located, so careful planning is suggested. The plaza's most striking feature is its bronze fountain with the statute of the Angel of Fame. The Plaza de Armas commemorates Peruvian independence.

The Lima Cathedral, completed in 1538, combines Baroque and neo-classical styles. Twin towers were added to the entrance in the 1790s. Francisco Pizarro himself placed the cathedral's first stone; not surprisingly, he is buried there in a chapel.

The most frequented church in Lima is the Church of Saint Francis of Assisi, built around 1674. The richly ornamented Baroque style was very popular when this and other buildings in Peru were built. The church has vast catacombs where an estimated 75,000 people are buried. There are so many bones in the burial area that they are stacked up like inventory in a macabre warehouse.

The Inquisition Museum is housed in a former mansion of the founding families of Lima; the mansion became the home of the Spanish Inquisition in Peru. While the museum is architecturally beautiful, it contains original jails and torture chambers in which heretics were tortured.

The National Museum of Art, built around 1872, exhibits a fine collection from pre-Columbian artifacts to Spanish colonial art. An important exhibit displays 2,000-year old weavings that were discovered in the area.

San Martín Plaza was inaugurated in 1921 to commemorate the 100th anniversary of Peruvian independence. Notable features include the statue of the general José de San Martín and the former hotel Bolivar, once the most fashionable in Lima. Visitors delight in the orange-colored facades of the surrounding buildings–somewhat unusual for Lima.

The Trivia

Fact: Pizarro referred to the city of Lima as the City of Kings. Early maps display both names, but Lima prevailed as the more common name.

Fact: Air pollution is a serious health issue in this ever-expanding city. Leaded gasoline is still used, and no restrictions are placed on either the age or condition of motorized vehicles.

Fact: The viceroy was the single most important person in Lima during the period of Spanish control; his authority equaled that of the Spanish kings. There is a legend that when a new viceroy first entered the city of Lima, the streets would be paved with silver bars, from the doors of the city to the viceroy's new home.

Fact: Lima and Peru went through a golden period in the late 1800s, curiously called the age of Guano. This natural fertilizer found on the Pacific coast became a lucrative export, mainly to Europe. The money generated during this era helped finance a series of civic improvements in Lima.

Fact: Lima is arranged in the manner of ancient Roman settlements, with 117 blocks surrounding the main square. Colonial institutions were built along the square's perimeter, including Pizarro's residence, restored in the 20th century and currently the seat of Peru's executive branch.

Fact: The Spanish established a strict class system in Peru, which endures in some form today. Under this system, an elite white upper class controlled the large native Indian lower class. In the early 1900s a middle class of whites and mestizos began to emerge.

Why Lima Is a *50 plus one* City

Lima represents both the grandeur (and the suffering) of its colonial past. Few cities in the world are so tied to the Spanish Empire. The city reflects the convergence of Spanish and Peruvian history and culture. At times chaotic and challenging, Lima is nevertheless a bastion of cultural and artistic greatness.

26

Lisbon, Portugal

The Basic Facts

Lisbon is the capital and largest city in Portugal. Almost a fifth of the country's people live in and around the city. After decades of economic instability, Lisbon has become a thriving center of Portugal's economy with a revitalized urban landscape.

Geography

Lisbon lies at 38 degrees 42 minutes north latitude and 9 degrees 5 minutes west longitude. The city a major European port, located in southwestern Portugal where the Tagus River empties into the Atlantic Ocean. Lisbon covers 32 square miles and is composed of many public squares, avenues and parks. Most areas of the city are hilly, with many streets too steep for automobiles, but the downtown area (the Baixa) near the harbor is flat.

Climate

Lisbon's climate is one of the warmest of any European city, thanks to the influence of the Gulf Stream. Average temperatures range from the upper 50s Fahrenheit in winter to the lower 80s Fahrenheit in summer. Spring and summer in Lisbon are usually sunny; autumn and winter are often quite rainy and windy.

Government

Portugal is divided into 22 districts, each with an elected governor and legislature. Cities and towns within each district also have their own local governments. A civil governor, appointed by the central government, is responsible for the district of Lisbon. The district is subdivided into municipalities, wards, and parishes. Parish representatives are elected locally and then elect the parish committee. Lisbon's Municipal Assembly, the legislative branch of the local government, includes parish committee representatives and those directly elected by the local citizens. The chamber is headed by a president appointed by the district governor.

Demographics

Lisbon is Portugal's largest and fastest-growing region. The area's first inhabitants were the Iberians, who settled more than 3,000 years ago. The population later expanded with an influx of peoples from eastern Europe, the Mediterranean and former African colonies. The current population includes all of these groups.

Economy

Trade is a major part of Lisbon's economy; ships travel through the Tagus estuary, one of Europe's most important natural harbors. Shipbuilding is a major industry in Lisbon, as is manufacturing. The city is also the center of Portugal's banking and commercial sectors.

The History

The earliest inhabitants of the area surrounding present-day Lisbon were the Iberians. The Celts invaded about 1000 B.C. and intermarried with the Iberians. Most scholars believe that Lisbon dates to pre-Roman days and that it was a constant battleground between the Phoenicians, Greeks and Carthaginians. Lisbon was the most important city in the western Iberian region during the time of Roman rule, which began in 205 B.C. After the Roman Empire collapsed, the area was ransacked by a series of northern European tribes until the area was seized by the Moors in 714 A.D.

In 1147, Christian forces led by Alfonso I wrested the city of Lisbon from Moorish control, and Alfonso I became Portugal's first king; Lisbon became the country's capital in 1255. Portugal's golden era of exploration began in the 15th century; one of the most famous Portuguese discoveries was that of Vasco da Gama, who navigated the first sea route to India.

Felipe II of Spain became king in 1580, and reigned for 60 years until nationalist Portuguese seized power. During that time, Brazil was a Portuguese territory; gold was discovered there in the 17th century and Lisbon enjoyed a brief economic boom. Some 60,000 to 90,000 people perished in 1755, when a major earthquake devastated the city.

Napoleon occupied the city briefly at the start of the 19th century. Following his defeat and withdrawal, the city and country spiraled into a lengthy period of political chaos. In 1926 António de Oliveira Salazar became prime minister of Portugal; he led an authoritarian regime until his overthrow in 1974. Lisbon and Portugal rose out of the squalor following Salazar's regime. With the help of the European Union, Lisbon has rebounded to become a thriving center of Portugal's economy.

The Sights and Sounds

Lisbon is small in comparison to other major European cities. Touring the city can be a challenge because the city is built on a series of hills. Distances can be deceptive because landmarks and sites are at different heights. Funicular railways and street elevators help visitors navigate the steep hills.

St. George Castle, a majestic structure in the heart of Lisbon, is architecturally significant for its Roman, Visigoth and Moorish influences. Beautiful gardens surround the structure. It is an ideal location from which to view the city from afar; travel nearby and explore the Alfama district.

Alfama surrounds St. George Castle in an area that roughly parallels that of the city's original Moorish settlement. Visitors find the district's white-washed houses and red-tiled roofs rather charming.

The Baixa is the city center; also called the lower town, it is an area home to crafts and trades including artists, street performers and metal smiths. The neighborhood reflects this tradition with a variety of shops selling traditional Portuguese wares. Cafes and restaurants line the area to ensure that everyone is well fed while wandering the Baixa.

The Calouste Gulbenkian Foundation displays classical paintings, fine porcelain, jewelry and other antiquities. Several specialty museums in Lisbon include the Puppet Museum, the Port Wine Institute–yes, samplings are provided–and the National Tile Museum.

A museum devoted exclusively to Portuguese art is the National Museum of Art. Housed in a grand 17th century palace, the collection emphasizes the finest art of Portugal from the 15th to 19th centuries.

Belém is an old quarter of Lisbon near the seacoast. Visitors come here to view the neighborhood's Gothic architecture, including the the Jerónimos Monastery. This historic structure was built in the 16th century over a period of 50 years, and commemorates Vasco da Gama's voyage to India. Also here is the Bélem Tower, which was built during the same period to defend the monastery and the nearby port of Bélem.

The Trivia

Fact: Although most historians believe Lisbon was founded by the Phoenicians, a popular legend has it that the city was founded by Ulysses, the famous Greek explorer. After the Romans gained control of the city, it was briefly named Felicitas Julia in honor of Julius Caesar.

Fact: Lisbon was a neutral city during World War II and was a safe haven for Europeans (especially Jews) seeking passage to America. The classic movie *Casablanca* focuses on a flight to Lisbon to escape Nazism and the government of Vichy France.

Fact: The Roman Catholic Church was effectively part of the Portuguese government until the two entities separated in 1911; nevertheless, Catholicism remains the predominate religion in Portugal. Devout pilgrims travel to the small town of Fátima each year to visit the Sanctuary of Fátima, where the Virgin Mary reportedly appeared to three peasant children in 1917.

Fact: In 1290 King Denis I founded the first university in Lisbon.

Fact: The westernmost point of continental Europe is located at Cabo da Roca, a cape overlooking the Atlantic Ocean west of Lisbon.

Fact: Fado is a Portuguese music genre reminiscent of the blues, expressing longing, lost lovers and sadness. Restaurants that feature this traditional music are generally upscale and the shows typically begin after 10 p.m.

Fact: Trams and funicular railways are Lisbon's primary modes of public transportation. The Tagus River is spanned by the 25th of April Bridge, one of the world's longest suspension bridges, and the Vasco de Gama Bridge, the longest bridge in Europe.

Why Lisbon Is a *50 plus one* City

Lisbon is a popular tourist destination for those interested in its colonial past, its history of exploration, and its cultural influences. Lisbon may be a relatively small city, but it is charming and delightful, and proudly displays its rich heritage.

27

London, England

The Basic Facts

London is the capital of the United Kingdom, which includes England, Wales and Northern Ireland. It is the largest city in the UK and one of the world's greatest cities, with an amazing mix of culture, commerce, and historic architecture and sites. London is also one of the world's oldest cities, and was originally a trading post for the Roman Empire around 43 A.D. The city was devastated during bombing raids in World War II, but reconstruction began soon afterward, giving the London skyline new and brilliant skyscrapers. The city hosts thousands of visitors every year, but still must deal with the problems of traffic congestion and pollution.

Geography

London lies at 51 degrees 30 minutes north latitude and 0 degrees 7 minutes west longitude. The city is located in the southeast of England and the Thames River flows through its center. The Thames connects London to the North Sea, enabling access to worldwide shipping routes.

The entire city covers 614 square miles and is divided into specific areas: the City Section, which includes London's financial center; the West End, which includes stores, nightlife, and the UK government center; and South Bank, a center of London culture with many art galleries, museums and theaters.

Residential areas, small offices and factories surround Central London, beyond which are less-crowded areas known to Londoners as the suburbs.

Climate

Although London is a northern city, it has a temperate climate thanks to the North Atlantic Drift of the Gulf Stream. Severe cold and warmth are uncommon; average winter temperatures are in the mid-40s Fahrenheit and summers average in the upper 60s to lower 70s Fahrenheit.

Contrary to popular belief, London's climate is not extraordinarily rainy or foggy. Rain is moderate throughout the year, and the demise of 19th century industry has eliminated the thick fogs for which London is famous (or infamous).

Government

London consists of 32 boroughs and the City of London. Each has its own council and mayor elected every 4 years. With the exception of police and fire departments and public transport, the borough councils control most aspects of their local government services.

The Greater London Authority controls citywide services, including police, fire and public transport. The authority is composed of a 25-member assembly and a mayor elected for 4 years.

The Court of Common Counsel governs the City Section, and consists of elected alderman, 100 non-elected council members and the Lord Mayor of London.

Demographics

Each borough has its own identity, and most Londoners identify themselves by the specific borough in which they live. By popular tradition, the only real residents of London are Cockneys, those born within earshot of the bells of St. Mary-le-Bow. London's present population, like many of the world's large cities, is a melting pot, drawing people from other parts of the UK and from around the world. Nearly seven million people call London home.

Economy

London is the driving force behind the UK's economy, with residents working in finance, government, trade, and national or local government. Major London industries include printing and publishing, clothing and textiles, electronics, food and pharmaceuticals. Even though London's trade has moved mostly from its ports to container shipping elsewhere, the city is the major conduit of trade from the nearby port city of Tilbury.

London is home to some of the world's greatest financial and insurance institutions. Tourism is a major industry for the city. London is also the base for most of England's communications industry, including the BBC.

The History

In the 5th century, the Romans left Britain to defend Rome from a Barbarian invasion. London quickly declined as most other inhabitants abandoned the city at this time. In the mid-1000s the city's population rebounded after Edward the Confessor built a palace and a monastery church on the Thames about two miles southwest of London. The modern city of Westminster is located around this site.

During the Middle Ages, many of London's most famous landmarks were created, including London Bridge and Old St. Paul's Cathedral. London became self-governing during this period. The city grew rapidly during the 16th and 17th centuries, especially under the rule of Henry VIII and Elizabeth I. In America's early years, London became an important trade center, a development that helped England assert its colonial control throughout the world.

The Great Plague and the Great Fire of London ravaged the city in the late 1600s. Puritans led by Oliver Cromwell seized power from King Charles I during this period and ruled both England and London. But by the 1800s, London was the largest city in the world, due largely to the advent of the Industrial Revolution. Many Londoners then moved to the suburbs that were growing in the outlying areas.

London experienced sporadic bomb damage during World War I, yet during World War II the city was devastated in an attack known as the Blitz. German bombers rained bombs on the city in an attempt to weaken Londoners' resolve. Much to Germany's chagrin, the Blitz empowered the city to rebuild.

The Sights and Sounds

To explore London is a massive undertaking, so you will need ample time to enjoy the city's sights and sounds. Although most of the art and architecture of London is concentrated in the city's two main sections (Westminster and the City of London), the geographic area is quite extensive. Government is centered in Westminster, and the City of London is the home of commerce, banking and business. If time and energy permit, visitors may want to include Covent Garden, Hyde Park, Kensington Gardens and the South Kensington museum district in their itinerary.

Buckingham Palace surely rates as one of the greatest sites in London. Many, however, consider the building's architecture to be rather average; one would expect the palace's exterior to be more opulent, as it is the home of the royal family. The monarchy and its administration are in residence for most of the year, and as a result, only parts of the palace are open for viewing during the summer months.

The Houses of Parliament stand in tribute to the British tradition of representative government. Visitors will enjoy the nearby Palace of Westminster; regrettably, however, the only parts of the original building still standing are the Jewel Tower (built around 1365) and Westminster Hall. The remainder of the building, including the chambers and committee rooms of Parliament, was rebuilt after a fire in 1834. Victoria Tower and St. Stephen's Tower flank the building on either end. The latter is formally known as the Clock Tower, and houses the famous bell affectionately known as Big Ben.

Nos. 10 and 11 Downing Street are famous addresses for British government and for the world at large. No. 10 is the official residence of the Prime Minister, and No. 11 contains the offices of the financial minister, the Chancellor of the Exchequer.

British monarchs are by tradition crowned in the most important church in all England: Westminster Abbey. This church, which dates from the 11th century, contains the Henry VII Chapel, one of the finest in Europe. Poets Corner, another historic part of the building, is the resting place of literary greats including Chaucer, Hardy, Dickens, Tennyson and Browning.

History buffs will enjoy a visit to the Cabinet War Rooms, perhaps not a popular spot on a London tour, but a fascinating one nevertheless. This underground bunker behind the Foreign Office was the nerve center for the British Empire during World War II. Winston Churchill and his cabinet met here to direct the war effort and were protected from the ravages of the Blitz. Today, the room appears as though the Prime Minister and his cabinet were about to arrive; time has left the room untouched and ready for action.

The British Museum is renowned for its collection of historically significant antiquities, including the priceless Elgin Marbles and the Rosetta Stone. No other museum in the world comes close to rivaling its collections. The Egyptian, Greek and Roman collections are without equal, and the Renaissance collection of art and artifacts is outstanding. The British Museum is enormous, requiring several visits to see all the exhibits. Another notable London museum is the National Gallery in Trafalgar Square, which houses countless important works of art between the 14th and 19th centuries.

St. Paul's Cathedral, completed around 1710, is the heart and soul of London. The famous architect, Christopher Wren, designed this imposing structure—he is buried there in tribute—and its impressive dome attracts visitors time and time again. The cathedral survived the Blitz as a memorial to faith, to the city of London, and to Christopher Wren. St. Paul's American Chapel pays tribute to the 28,000 U.S. servicemen who lost their lives in World War II.

The Tower of London, built in the 11th century, is perhaps the strangest building in all England. Today the tower houses the Crown Jewels, but it formerly served as a fortress and a palace. Visitors, however, flock to the tower for its historical significance as a prison and a place of execution. The area around the tower is a complex of buildings that comprised the old medieval palace.

Trivia

Fact: During the 1950s, Londoners dealt with deadly smog caused by coal smoke from homes and private industry. Four thousand Londoners died in 1952 during a particularly deadly smog event, after which Parliament passed clean air acts limiting coal-smoke emissions in the city.

Fact: Until 1750, London's only link with its South Bank was the original London Bridge. Westminster Bridge was completed in 1750 and many other bridges were built in later years.

Fact: The London theater scene, which is still thriving today, began during the reign of Elizabeth I, a noted patron of the arts. The theaters attracted such unruly crowds that they were actually located outside the city walls. One of the most famous theaters was the Globe, where many of William Shakespeare's plays debuted. The original Globe Theatre was demolished in 1644, but a replica located near the original site opened in 1997 to great acclaim.

Why London Is a *50 plus one* City

London was a Roman city that has become a seat of government and a major world financial center. It is truly one of the most impressive cities, known for its size, its vitality, and its marvelous historical significance. London was and remains a city of the world for all to enjoy.

28

Madrid, Spain

The Basic Facts

Madrid is the capital of Spain and the country's largest city. The city was founded by the Moors in the 9th century. After the fall of the Spanish fascist government in the late 1900s, Madrid underwent rapid growth helped by developing industries and extensive building programs.

Geography

Madrid lies at 40 degrees 26 minutes north latitude and 3 degrees 42 minutes west longitude. The city is located on a high plateau near the geographic center of Spain. At an altitude of 2,150 feet, it is one of the highest European capitals. In the 1950s Madrid experienced a population boom, and since then has expanded to include residential and industrial suburbs. Madrid covers almost 234 square miles.

Climate

Madrid has a Mediterranean climate. Average temperatures range from the mid-40s Fahrenheit in winter to the upper 80s Fahrenheit in summer. Rainfall is limited throughout the year and summers tend to be very dry.

Government

Spain is divided into autonomous communities that have authority over the government services within those communities. Madrid is the capital of the Autonomous Community of Madrid and consists of a single province.

The city of Madrid has an elected city council and mayor. Each member of the city council also serves as an administrator for a particular part of the city government. The Autonomous Community of Madrid has an elected regional parliament, which elects a president to lead the regional government. The president is assisted by ministers who oversee the community's administrative services.

Demographics

Madrid residents are officially known as Madrilenos, but they are colloquially called gatos (cats). Madrilenos speak Castilian Spanish, the official language of Spain. Most residents live in apartments, and the city is rather crowded.

In the late 20th century, the city's actual population decreased due to suburban flight; recent immigration has reversed that trend. The current population numbers about three million people. Major immigrant groups include Ecuadorians, Peruvians, Colombians, Moroccans, Chinese, Guineans, Romanians and Filipinos.

Economy

Madrid's economy has historically focused on the national government. In the 1900s, an effort was made to increase Madrid's industrial base, and today the city is second only to Barcelona in terms of manufacturing. Major industries include automobiles, chemicals, clothing and electronics. A significant portion of the economy depends on tourism; Madrid is one of the most popular tourist attractions in Europe.

The History

The Moors built a fortress called Majerit on the site that would eventually become the city of Madrid. King Alfonso VI of Leon and Castile ousted the Moors from the area in 1085, but Madrid remained a small town until 1561, when Philip II moved the court to Madrid, essentially making it the capital of Spain.

In the 15th and 16th centuries, as the Spanish Empire grew in power and Spain's explorers discovered treasures in the Americas, Madrid flourished and became one of western Europe's great cities. Although the city was home to rich aristocrats and powerful royal officials, most of the city residents lived in poverty. At the time, Madrid was not considered a safe city due to frequent epidemics and a skyrocketing crime rate. The government took steps to clean up the city in the 1700s; conditions substantially improved for the population as a whole.

Napoleon occupied the city from 1808 to 1813 until a growing Spanish resistance movement drove the French from Spain. Madrid did not join the Industrial Revolution of the late 18th and early 19th centuries. As a result, Madrid's population decreased at a time when industrialized cities in Europe experienced a population boom. Madrid languished until the 1930s when the city became pivotal in the Spanish Civil War. The government-supporting Spanish Republicans moved the capital from Madrid to Valencia and then to Barcelona, but when the fascists under General Francisco Franco won the war in 1939, Madrid was re-established as the nation's capital. After the war, industrial growth helped to improve Madrid's economic situation. Spain was officially a neutral country during World War II.

The Sights and Sounds

The Royal Palace is an excellent first destination. It is said that Philip V, the first Bourbon King of Spain, designed the building in the manner of the gardens and buildings of Versailles. No expense was spared in the construction of this magnificent 2,800 room palace. The palace was built between 1738 and 1755 on the site of a former Moorish fortress named Antiguo Alcázar. Spanish monarchs lived in the palace from from 1764 to 1931. The sheer size of the palace, its lavish decorations, and its elaborate Rococo splendor make this one of Madrid's finest tourist sites. The adjoining gardens, not surprisingly, are some of the best in Madrid. The palace is no longer the residence of the king, but is used for state functions and diplomatic receptions.

The Queen Sophia Arts Centre, which opened in 1986, is one of the most recent additions to the already impressive Madrid arts scene. One of the most famous works here is Picasso's Guernica. This painting, which captures the brutality and despair of war, depicts the Nazi bombing of the Basque city of Guernica. The center also includes important works by the Spanish painters Joan Miró and Salvador Dalí. The permanent collection is divided between the second and fourth floors of the museum. The division intentionally separates works created before and after 1939, the end of the Spanish Civil War.

The Convent of the Royal Barefoot Nuns, which remains active to this day, dates to the time of Charles V, a Holy Roman Emperor and King of Spain in the 16th century. The nuns who entered this convent were royals from the courts of Spain and its empire. For this reason, the convent holds a treasure-trove of art, paintings, religious artifacts and tapestries, most of which are on display to the public.

The Prado Museum is considered one of the finest museums of its kind in the world, housing a virtual history of Spanish art and culture. Magnificent works from Goya and El Greco are just the beginning. It is difficult to see all the museum has to offer, even in a day or two. There are some 8,600 paintings alone, along with many sculptures, drawings and other art.

If there is anything missing from the Prado collection, visitors will find it at the Thyssen Bornemisza Museum of Art, a collection of some 800 paintings from the 13th through the 20th century. This collection was acquired by Spain from a Swiss baron; the museum is named in his honor.

Visitors and locals alike love the Sunday morning market at El Rastro Flea Market. The market has been in business for nearly 5 centuries. Vendors sell all kinds of goods and there are many excellent tapas restaurants nearby.

One of the most magnificent buildings in Madrid is the Palace of Bibliotecas y Museos. It was built in 1892 to celebrate the 400th anniversary of Columbus's discovery of America and to honor his Spanish patron, Queen Isabella II. It now houses the Archaeological Museum as well as the National Library and Art Galleries.

Madrid's Great Square is an architecture marvel and gathering place. King Philip III established the square in 1619; in tribute to him, there is a statue of Philip III on horseback in the middle of the square. Throughout history this place has been the site of canonizations, hangings, riots, bullfights and just about every other social gathering.

Madrid, and all of Spain for that matter, is especially known for bullfighting and flamenco dancing. Bullfighting takes place at the Plaza La Ventas, usually on Sundays between March and October. Traditional flamenco dancers, graceful and expressive, frequently perform in the city's nightclubs.

The Trivia

Fact: The Madrilenos, residents of Madrid, have a leisurely lifestyle. Many offices and stores open at 9 a.m. and close at 1:30 p.m. for lunch. Businesses usually reopen at 5 p.m. and close again around 8 p.m.

Fact: Football (known as soccer in America) is Spain's national passion. Real Madrid is the local football team and one of the most beloved world teams.

Fact: Visitors may be surprised to note that dinner typically does not start until around 10 p.m. In fact, traffic jams are a common occurrence in the early morning, when revelers return home from a night of fun.

Why Madrid Is a *50 plus one* City

Imagine a city with nearly 500 years of wealth accumulated from far-flung and culturally rich colonies. This is Madrid in a nutshell, defined by its artistic, religious, architectural and cultural heritage. Visitors come to this fine European city to be both entertained and educated.

29

Mecca, Saudi Arabia

The Basic Facts

Mecca is the holiest city of Islam and the birthplace of the prophet Muhammad. One of the Five Pillars of Islam requires that every Muslim who is physically and financially able must make a pilgrimage to Mecca (known as the hajj) at least once.

Geography

Mecca lies at 21 degrees 27 minutes north latitude and 39 degrees 45 minutes east longitude. The city is located in western Saudi Arabia in a barren valley surrounded by hills and mountains. The heart of Mecca is the Kaaba within the Sacred Mosque. The Kaaba is a black granite structure, one of the most sacred sites in Islam; Muslims throughout the world face the direction of the Kaaba during their daily prayers.

In the 1950s, modern housing was built in the city for permanent residents and hotels for hajj pilgrims. Suburbs sprang up around the city for wealthier residents.

Climate

Mecca's climate is similar to the rest of Saudi Arabia: arid and quite warm throughout the year. Average temperatures range from the mid-80s Fahrenheit in winter to the upper 90s Fahrenheit in summer.

Government

Saudi Arabia is ruled by a king with the assistance of appointed ministers. The country is divided into 13 regions. Each region has a regional governor in charge of government services. The governor reports directly to the Saudi Arabian Minister of the Interior.

Demographics

The population of Mecca is almost entirely Middle Eastern and numbers about 1.1 million people. Many residents are employed year-round solely to prepare for and manage the activities of the annual hajj, which attracts millions of Muslims from around the world. During the hajj, roadblocks are set up to keep non-Muslims from entering Mecca. In fact, non-Muslims are prohibited from entering the city at any time. This has not prevented some non-Muslims from secretly participating in the hajj and writing about their experiences.

Economy

Mecca's economy depends almost entirely on the money spent by hajj pilgrims. The Saudi Arabian government invests millions of dollars every year to help the city provide adequate security, health care and other services. There are small industries located in Mecca, but the city itself has not been a significant contributor to the Saudi Arabian economy since the 1940s.

The Madinah al-Munawarah Highway is the principal road serving Mecca. Rail travel is almost nonexistent in Saudi Arabia. The King Abdul Aziz International Airport in nearby Jiddah is the principal airport for international pilgrims making the hajj.

The History

Abraham, the patriarch of the Israelites, is said to have arrived in Mecca as early as 3000 B.C. According to Islamic tradition, Abraham left Mecca on God's command, leaving his wife and son there to die. Abraham later returned and according to tradition, God commanded him to create the Kabaa.

Mecca began as a trading center in about 500 A.D. The residents gradually moved away from the monotheism practiced by Abraham and became monotheistic; they worshipped their idols at the Kaaba. The prophet Muhammad was born in Mecca in 570, but was driven from the city in 622 after its people rejected his teachings. In 630 AD, Muhammad and his followers returned to take Mecca by force. They destroyed the pagan idols, but left the shrine of the Kabaa intact. Shortly after his return, Muhammad instituted the ritual of the hajj and declared the city the center of Islam.

Although Mecca remained a holy city, its political influence in the Middle East declined rapidly in the 7th century. Mecca was ruled until 1924 by the descendants of Muhammad known as Sharifs. In that year, the Arab leader, Abd al-Aziz ibn Saud conquered the city and it became part of the Kingdom of Saudi. The city grew rapidly in the latter half of the 20th century and attracts thousands of the world's Muslims during the annual hajj.

The Sights and Sounds

Pilgrims end their hajj at the Sacred Mosque (Masjid al-Haram), where they recite prayers and perform various rituals over a period of several days. One of these rituals involves circling the Kaaba seven times.

Kaaba is the holy shrine at Mecca that houses a sacred religious relic. Muslims believe that this shrine was built by Abraham and his son Ishmael. It is thought to be the first place created on the planet and a place so sacred that God's power directly touches the Earth at this point.

The Well of Zamzam is another holy site in Mecca. The water from this well is believed to have healing properties. Most Muslim visitors bring a large bottle of this holy water back home with them.

Pilgrims also visit a village close to Mecca called Mina. There they perform another sacred ritual called stoning the devil. To symbolize this ritual, Mina has a number of stone columns in the village. After visiting the village of Mina, pilgrims walk up a hill called the Mount Arafat to pray. This site was where the prophet Muhammad delivered his final sermon.

Medina, near Mecca, is also off-limits to non-Muslims. Medina is the second holiest city of Islam because it is the former home of Muhammad and also where he died. The first Islamic mosque is also located in Medina. Pilgrims who visit Mecca also visit Medina during the hajj.

The Trivia

Fact: Saudi Arabia is an Islamic country and has strict rules regarding the manner in which women can dress and behave. Female visitors are advised to dress modestly in long shirts, long skirts and headscarves. Passersby often comment raucously if they see an improperly-dressed woman.

Fact: Experts advise that a woman should travel to Mecca—and elsewhere in Saudi Arabia, for that matter—with her husband or another male relative, in order to spare themselves from unnecessary trouble with locals. Women are also strongly recommended never to walk unattended.

Fact: The Kaaba stands within the Sacred Mosque and contains the Black Stone, which Muslims believe was sent from heaven by Allah and discovered by Muhammad. Many contemporary scholars believe this stone is in fact a meteorite.

Fact: According to Arab tradition, after they were cast out from Eden, Adam and Eve eventually came to Mount Arafat, near Mecca. Adam prayed to God to let him build a shrine in Mecca. According to legend, Adam is buried in Mecca and Eve is buried in nearby Jiddah.

Fact: The pilgrimage of the hajj is one of five fundamental Islamic practices known as the Five Pillars of Islam. Before commencing the hajj, the pilgrim must redress all wrongs, pay off all debts, and have enough money both for the journey and to support his or her family while away.

Why Mecca Is a *50 plus one* City

Mecca's greatness results not from its tourism, and certainly not for its nightlife. Mecca is a great city because it a holy city, the holiest in all Islam. Most westerners simply cannot comprehend the significance of this city for worldwide Muslims. During the hajj the city is chaotic and crowded, but for the devout it is a religious experience that cannot be equaled.

30

Mexico City, Mexico

The Basic Facts

Mexico City, the capital of Mexico, is one of the largest cities in the world. The city experienced an economic boom from the 1940s to 1970, which caused an influx of immigrants and contributed to the overcrowding problems the city experiences today.

Geography

Mexico City lies at 19 degrees 28 minutes north latitude and 99 degrees 9 minutes west longitude. Mexico City is built on ground that used to be the lake bed of Lake Texcoco in central Mexico, roughly halfway between the Gulf of Mexico and the Pacific Ocean. The city sits in a natural basin almost 1.5 miles above sea level. The city covers roughly 600 square miles and the metropolitan area, including parts of the state of Mexico to the north.

Climate

Mexico City is 7,349 feet above sea level. This altitude makes Mexico City much cooler than the nearby coastal areas. However, visitors to Mexico City may initially be short of breath until they grow accustomed to the thinner air. Temperatures are moderate and consistent throughout the year; average temperatures range from the upper 60s in winter to the mid-70s in summer. Mexico City is mostly dry during the year, but there can be unexpected afternoon showers in the summer. Apart from the thin air, visitors to Mexico City should be aware of another aspect of its climate: the high level of air pollution and smog resulting from the city's overcrowding and traffic congestion.

Government

Mexico City has the same official boundaries as the Federal District (Distrito Federal, or D.F.) of Mexico, which is a separate political area governed similarly to the United States' District of Columbia.

Mexico City's mayor (whose official title is Jefe de Gobierno, or head of government) is the chief official of the D.F. The mayor is elected to a 6-year term and is considered second in power only to the president of Mexico.

Voters also elect a legislative assembly of 66 deputies representing city wards, as well as senators and deputies from the D.F. to serve in Mexico's General Congress.

Demographics

The majority of Mexico City residents are mestizos, descendants of the native Indians and the Spanish settlers who arrived in the 1500s. Almost all residents are Spanish-speaking; roughly 2 percent also speak an Indian language. The promise of good paying jobs and economic opportunities has drawn many rural Mexicans to Mexico City. Recent European, Middle Eastern, and Asian immigration has given the city an international flavor. Roman Catholicism is the dominant religion. The population numbers more than 8.7 million, but the entire metropolitan area's population is over 19 million, making it one of the largest metropolitan areas in the world.

Economy

Almost half of Mexico's manufacturing industry is located in or around Mexico City. Many workers also work in the petroleum, mineral refining and construction industries. The city and the federal government are also major employers. Mexico City is the country's center for finance and telecommunications. An interesting media fact is that 14 newspapers are published daily in the city—more per capita than any other world city.

The History

The Aztec city of Tenochtitlán was founded in 1325 on the site that would become Mexico City. Emperor Montezuma welcomed the Spanish explorer Hernándo Cortés into the city in 1519, believing him to be a representative of the Aztec god Quetzalcoatl. Cortés promptly took control of the city, but was forced out a year later. He returned with a larger force in 1521, reclaimed the city and destroyed it. Cortés then directed the construction of Mexico City on the site, and declared it the capital of New Spain. The city soon became the largest city in the Western Hemisphere. After a disastrous flood in 1629, the Spanish created canal and dike systems to drain Lake Texcoco.

In 1810 Mexico declared independence from Spain, and Mexico City remained the capital. In 1847, during the Mexican-American War, U.S. troops invaded and besieged Mexico City until 1848. France conquered Mexico City in 1863 and Maximilian—of the Austrian Habsburg family—became emperor of Mexico. Maximilian was deposed by General Porfirio Díaz, who became the country's president in 1876 and ruled as a dictator. Discontent grew, however, and Díaz was jailed in 1910, an event that brought about the Mexican Revolution. Many groups would fight for control of the city over the next several decades.

The Sights and Sounds

The heart of the historical and traditional section of Mexico City is the Centro Histórico. Several important museums in this area are frequent stops for visitors, including the Antiguo Colegio de San Ildefonso, built originally as a Catholic college in the 18th century. The museum features exhibits of regional artists. In addition, Museo de la Ciudad de México, the city museum, houses a fine collection devoted almost exclusively to the history of Mexico City. Visitors also enjoy the Museo Cuevas, which honors the work of José Luis Cuevas and other modern artists from around the world.

The Church of Santo Domingo, built in the 18th century, is a fine example of the Baroque style so popular at the time the church and other buildings were constructed. Alameda Central is nearby: a large and scenic park filled with fountains, lush landscaping, and often crowded with locals and visitors alike. This area had once been an Aztec market.

Mexico City's Zócalo, or the main square, is a huge space devoted largely to spectacular events: Independence Day celebrations, festivals and political rallies. This area was once the ceremonial center of the Aztec empire; later, the Spanish constructed marvelous buildings in this area.

The Cathedral Metropolitan took nearly 3 centuries to complete; like most cathedrals completed over so many years, it reflects the various styles of architecture of many different eras. The church is filled with art, artifacts and altars–an amazing collection, among the finest in the Spanish Empire. Concern for the structural integrity of the church recently spurred rehabilitative efforts; it was sinking under its own weight.

The Palacio National is at the site of Montezuma's former castle. This palace was built under the direction of Hernándo Cortés in the 17th century; additions were constructed in the 20th century. It is the seat of government and houses the famous liberty bell, first rung by Miguel Hidalgo in 1810 to proclaim Mexico's independence. Murals painted by the famous Mexican artist Diego Rivera dominate the palace; these murals depict more than 200 years of Mexican history, and took more than 15 years to complete.

Museo de Templo Mayor is a large museum built on the former location of the Great Temple of Tenochtitlán. A notable feature is the temple dedicated to the ancient Aztec gods Huitzilopochtli and Tlaloc, representing death and rain, respectively. Thousands of people are said to have been sacrificed to the gods at this spot. The adjacent museum contains thousands of historical artifacts (including skulls, carvings, and ceramic) that were discovered here and at other central Mexican ruins. The museum's pièce de résistance is the Coyolxauhqui Stone, an eight-ton carving named for the Moon goddess who was beheaded for slaughtering hundreds of her people. Cheery group, these Aztecs!

The Museo Nacional de Antropología is considered one of the world's greatest anthropological museums, with its outstanding collection of Aztec and Mayan art as well as artifacts of other Mexican cultures. The museum is in Chapultepec Park, along with others including the Museum of Modern Art and the Tamayo Museum of Contemporary Art.

The Trivia

Fact: Most of historical Mexico City was built by native Mexicans, the slaves of New Spain. Rubble from the original Aztec city was used to construct much of the city.

Fact: A major earthquake struck Mexico City in September 1985. The earthquake and its aftershocks destroyed more than 100,000 dwellings. The damage was so extensive due to the underlying soft clay. Survivors described the buildings as shaking like jelly. Following the earthquake, city officials instituted major reforms of city building codes and other safety measures. Official reports declared that 5,000 people were killed; unofficially, however, the death toll was estimated at nearly 50,000. As many as 90,000 people were rendered homeless.

Fact: Mexico City was besieged by U.S. troops in the Mexican-American War after the Battle of Chapultepec. In 1847 six military students jumped to their deaths from Chapultepec Castle to avoid having to surrender. The Monumento a los Niños (Monument to the Young Heroes) stands in their honor in Chapultepec Park.

Fact: Residents do not refer to the city as Mexico City. Rather, they call it either Mexico or D.F., the latter as an abbreviation for Distrito Federal.

Fact: Mexico City suffers greatly from air pollution due to population density, traffic congestion, and it location in a natural basin. The skies are often overcast with a thick brown smog, at which time the government officially declares dangerous pollution levels.

Why Mexico City Is a *50 plus one* City

Mexico City's expanse can be intimidating for visitors, but that feeling can be overcome by taking ample time to explore the city's sights and sounds. One cannot help to be impressed by the rich history, culture and vitality of this marvelous North American city. Viva la Ciudad!

31

Montreal, Canada

The Basic Facts

Montreal is one of the world's largest French-speaking cities. It is also largest city in the province of Quebec and the second largest city in Canada. In the late 20th century high-tech industries came to dominate Montreal's economy.

Geography

Montreal lies at 45 degrees 30 minutes north latitude and 73 degrees 35 minutes west longitude. Montreal is located on the triangular Island of Montreal in southwestern Quebec, at the confluence of the St. Lawrence and Ottawa Rivers. The city is named after Mount Royal–actually a large hill, being roughly 700 feet tall–which lies due north of the city center. The Greater Montreal Area includes the city itself, Laval, Longueuil, and smaller neighboring cities.

Both the St. Lawrence River and Lachine Canal have served Montreal as important commercial and industrial corridors. The canal once served as a detour around the St. Lawrence's Lachine Rapids, but is no longer used for commercial shipping.

Climate

Montreal lies at the nexus of several climactic regions, so the weather can vary greatly day by day and even during the course of a single day. Montreal receives almost seven feet of snow during the winter and is rainy throughout the year. Due to its far northern location, winters in Montreal can be very cold with temperatures averaging in the lower 20s Fahrenheit. Summer is usually sunny, with temperatures averaging in the mid-70s Fahrenheit.

Government

In 2002 the Quebec provincial legislature enacted a law to combine Montreal with several surrounding municipalities; the city of Montreal now has 27 boroughs. The city is led by a mayor and a city council, whose members are elected from each borough. Elected officials serve 4-year terms.

Demographics

French is the dominant language of Montrealers; nearly 70 percent of residents speak French as a first language. Most street signs, therefore, are in French. Almost half of Montreal residents speak French and English, 35 percent speak only French, and 10 percent speak only English. Over 50 percent of Montrealers claim French ancestry. The city's population is roughly 1.5 million, and the population of the Greater Montreal Area is more than 3.5 million.

Economy

Montreal is a major hub for Canadian transportation, finance and manufacturing industries. Agriculture is important in the surrounding area, and thus food processing is an important component of Montreal's economy. Manufacturing industries are numerous, including aircraft and aircraft parts, telecommunications equipment, pharmaceuticals and other chemicals, clothing, and tobacco products. Montreal's high-tech industry has grown significantly in recent years.

The History

The Huron, Algonquin and Iroquois lived here for thousands of years—well before 1535, when the French explorer Jacques Cartier arrived. Samuel de Champlain established a fur trading post on the island in 1611, which was attacked repeatedly by the Iroquois. The Iroquois fiercely defended their land until 1701, when they signed a peace treaty with the French colonists. By the early 1700s, the city became known as Montreal and was the heart of France's North American empire. The British captured the city during the French and Indian War.

In 1763 the Treaty of Paris ended the war and Canada became a British colony. The city grew through the 18th and 19th century, largely due to British migration. Montreal also served as the capital of the United Province of Canada from 1844 to 1849.

The Sights and Sounds

Montreal is an old city in a new skin. Visitors can wander narrow cobblestone streets in Vieux-Montréal (the Old City) or enjoy the latest in haute couture downtown on Rue Ste.-Catherine. The city has much to offer year-round. The Underground City, an amazingly large collection of walkways, shops and restaurants, is a temperature-controlled option for winter visitors. Mount Royal affords four season sports including downhill and cross-country skiing, skating, biking and hiking.

Vieux Montréal contains most of the oldest structures and most romantic restaurants in the city. Cobblestone streets are lined with interesting antique shops, restaurants and cafes. In the summer, couples sip wine outside and watch the passing crowd. It is not uncommon to see street performers in this section of the city.

Visitors marvel at how far they feel from the city when in Mount Royal Park, which surrounds its namesake. The park, which covers about 490 acres, offers beautiful views of the cityscape. A 100-foot iron cross is lighted at night and provides a beautiful view from below.

Le Jardin Botanique de Montréal is the second largest botanical garden in the world, after London's Kew Gardens. Thousands of varieties of flowers and plants from around the world are showcased here. One highlight is the Chinese Garden featuring ponds, statues and plantings common to authentic gardens in China. The Insectarium de Montréal displays collections that include thousands of insects. Visit the delightful Butterflies Go Free Exhibit, where patrons can interact with thousands of wild butterflies in a simulated natural habitat.

Of all the Gothic churches in Montreal, the Notre-Dame de Montréal Basilica is a must-see. The architecture hearkens back to the centuries-old cathedrals of Europe, and its grand interior blends ornamentation with color in a dazzling display. Its stained-glass windows represent the city's rich history. Stars made of gold adorn the rich blue ceiling, and visitors often imagine stars shining in the heavens. The enormous organ contains nearly 7,000 pipes!

Summer is festival season in Montreal. In July the city hosts some of the best jazz musicians in the world at the International Jazz Festival. The World Film Festival screens great movies from around the globe in July and August. The Just For Laughs Comedy Festival and museum offers a unique insight into the definition of humor and how culture helps determine what is considered funny.

Montreal is home to the world-famous Cirque de Soleil, a modern humans-only circus. Its amazing and entertaining shows feature acrobats who contort themselves into unbelievable poses. The circus attracts tourists and locals alike.

The Stewart Museum, located on Île Sainte-Hélène near Montreal, provides an interesting glimpse into colonial life in the area. Permanent collections include the History Gallery, the Gunsmith's Gallery, and the 18th Century Physics Cabinet. Summer activities include a re-enactment of colonial life, 18th century military drills, and the Noonday Gun Salute.

Le Centre Canadien d'Architecture contains a variety of interactive exhibits on Canadian architecture, as well as multimedia presentations on architecture unique to Montreal. The building itself is unique in its design and structure.

The Trivia

Fact: A local ordinance requires that all companies having more than 50 employees must use French as their official business language.

Fact: Montreal was briefly occupied by American forces during the Revolutionary War. Despite the repeated efforts of Benjamin Franklin and other American diplomats to join the war against the British, French Canadians refused to do so, seeing the war as just a quarrel between Britain and her colonies.

Fact: The violence of the separatist movement included the kidnappings in 1970 of British trade commissioner James R. Cross and Quebec Labor minister Pierre LaPorte by separatist terrorists. Cross was released after the Canadian government guaranteed the kidnappers safe passage to Cuba. LaPorte was not as fortunate: he was killed while in custody.

Fact: One of the world's most unusual apartment developments is in Montreal. Called Habitat 67, it contains 158 apartments arranged like a stack of concrete boxes, with one apartment's roof serving as the terrace of another apartment. The complex was built for the 1967 World Fair.

Why Montreal Is a *50 plus one* City

Montreal has an old-world feel unlike most other North American cities. Its French influences and its French-speaking population may seem out of step with other Canadian cities, but that is part of its charm. Visitors enjoy exploring its art, architecture, nightlife, and colonial history.

32

Moscow, Russia

The Basic Facts

Moscow is the capital of Russia and the former capital of the USSR. The city dominates Russia's government, economy, industry, science and culture. Moscow was pivotal in the collapse of the Soviet Union, when Communist hardliners attempted a coup against President Mikhail Gorbachev. Russia now has a democratically elected government.

Geography

Moscow lies at 55 degrees 45 minutes north latitude and 37 degrees 37 minutes east longitude. The city is named after the Moscow River on which it is located, in European west-central Russia. The modern city has a wheel-shaped arrangement, which stems from its early history as a fortified city. Wide boulevards that extend from the center of the city make up the spokes of the wheel, and circular boulevards make up the inner and outer rims of the wheel.

Climate

Moscow's has a continental climate with warm summers and very cold winters. Average temperatures range from the lower 20s Fahrenheit in winter to the lower 70s Fahrenheit in summer.

Government

Moscow is one of two federal cities in Russia (St. Petersburg is the other); as such, the city operates as a region separate from Russian republics and other administrative divisions. Moscow is divided into 10 administrative districts that are subdivided into 125 municipal districts. The city is governed by a mayor, a vice-mayor and a 35-member Duma (city council); all are elected to 4-year terms. The mayor also appoints a first-deputy and deputy mayor, as well as prefects, who administer the 10 administrative districts.

Demographics

Muscovites, the residents of Moscow, speak the Russian language and use a modern form of the Cyrillic alphabet. For example, Moscow is spelled Мосва and pronounced moskva in English. Russians constitute the majority of the city's population; other nationalities represented include Ukraine, Belarus and Armenia. The city has no distinct ethnic neighborhoods. The city government has sought to limit the population in recent years due to a lack of affordable, quality housing. Even so, Moscow is a huge city by any standard: some 10.5 million people live in the city itself.

Economy

Many city residents are employed in the city and federal governments. Since the fall of the Soviet Union, most businesses in Moscow are privately owned, and the number of foreign businesses has risen. Moscow is the core of the Russian economy; industries include automobiles, buses, chemicals, dairy products, electrical equipment, steel, textiles and building materials. Russian communications are centered in Moscow, and the national newspaper Izvestia is headquartered here.

The History

Moscow was first mentioned in Russian chronicles in 1147 as a small town. In 1237 and 1238, invading Mongols killed the inhabitants and demolished the town. By the 14th century, however, the town rebounded and eventually became the capital of the Vladimir-Suzdal principality. The city's growth was attributed to its proximity to important land and water trade routes. In 1380, the Russian army defeated the Mongols in the Battle of Kulikovo. Tatars controlled the city during much of the 15th century, but in 1480 they were forced out by Ivan the Great.

In 1547, at the age of 16, Ivan the Terrible was crowned the first czar of Russia; Moscow became the country's capital. During the next century a succession of czars built the palaces of the Kremlin, mansions, churches and monasteries, thus greatly expanding the city and developing its industry. Although Peter the Great moved the Russian capital to St. Petersburg in 1712, Moscow remained the center of commerce and culture. Muscovites left the city when Napoleon invaded in 1812, but not before burning most of it to the ground. Moscow was quickly rebuilt following Napoleon's retreat that winter.

By the mid-1800s, Moscow regained its status as a transportation and industrial center and the population grew rapidly. Moscow became the capital of Russia once again following the Bolshevik revolution against czarist rule. German bombs heavily damaged Moscow during World War II, but following the war the city more than doubled in size.

The Sights and Sounds

Moscow is an old city with fascinating sights around every corner. From the old Soviet-era décor of the GUM department store to the modern apartment complexes on the edge of the city, Moscow is a city of endless possibilities. Muscovites are generally friendly toward Westerners, and since the dissolution of the USSR Moscow has been a popular tourist destination. Residents are often the best source of information on the city's finest sights and sounds.

No visit to Moscow is complete without a tour of the Kremlin. This massive fortified building, once the seat of supreme czarist power, is now the official residence of the President of the Russian Federation. The Armoury building, located in the northwestern section of the Kremlin, is a museum dedicated to Russian imperial treasures, as well as an impressive collection of priceless Faberge eggs.

St. Basil's Cathedral, or the Cathedral of St. Basil the Blessed, is a Moscow icon. It is recognized the world over, known as the church with the colorful onion domes.

The Kremlin and St. Basil's Cathedral are both located in Red Square, the central square of Moscow and home to annual parades and celebrations. You simply cannot visit Moscow without stopping in Red Square to admire its grandeur. Many visitors frequently line up at Lenin's Mausoleum, where the body of the former Bolshevik leader is still on display.

GUM (pronounced goom) department store is on the east side of Red Square and is the largest of its kind in Russia. Under Communist rule the center was owned by the federal government, but today it is privately owned. There are some 150 stores here, including a variety of high- and medium-fashion shops and a café; most Muscovites, however, cannot afford to purchase many of the items on display. The building's architecture and its central fountain are worth a look even if you do not feel like shopping.

One of the most impressive theaters in the world is Moscow's Bolshoi. Best known for its world-famous Bolshoi Ballet, the theatre also stages operas and concerts. The theater's architecture and décor are beautiful, especially at night.

The State Historical Museum is also in Red Square. It is the largest and most extensive Russian historical museum; its exhibitions span prehistory to the present day and include millions of Russian relics and artifacts.

Many Westerners, especially film buffs, are attracted to Gorky Park. This 300-acre amusement park includes cafes, a towering Ferris wheel, children's play areas, thrill rides and entertainment venues. Gorky Park is a fine place to escape the city and take in some people watching.

The Pushkin Museum of Fine Arts is located on Volkhonka Street and is a haven for art lovers. Exhibits run the gamut from ancient civilizations to Post-Impressionism.

Moscow is famous for the Great Moscow State Circus, a five-ring circus located on Tsvetnoi Boulevard. The amphitheatre in this dome-shaped structure is over 100 feet tall and seats 3,400. Visitors enjoy the elaborate shows that stage excellent acrobatics and animal acts.

The Trivia

Fact: Moscow is surrounded by acres of trees and parks known as the Green Belt.

Fact: One of the major pastimes in Moscow is playing chess. Russia's greatest chess champions have come from this city.

Fact: Russians are a very polite people. If you visit a house or apartment, it is customary to bring a small gift such as flowers or a bottle of wine or vodka. If you bring flowers, make sure to bring an odd number. Many Russians are a bit superstitious; even numbers of flowers are only put on graves.

Fact: Moscow was the center of two key battles in the country's history. The Russians ousted Napoleon's forces from the city–a success that inspired Tchaikovsky's 1812 Overture. In 1941 the German army was stopped outside the city, a fact which many historians credit with changing the course of World War II.

Fact: Moscow was the first Russian city to host the Summer Olympics in 1980. The United States and some 60 other nations boycotted the Olympics to protest the 1979 Soviet invasion of Afghanistan.

Fact: The Kremlin occupies 68 acres in the city center and is the seat of the Russian government.

Why Moscow Is a *50 plus one* City

Moscow experienced a tremendous resurgence following the collapse of the Soviet Union; it is now a popular destination for adventurous tourists. Stand in front of the Kremlin and imagine just for a moment being a part of Moscow's glorious history. Moscow's notable Russian architecture, its resilient people, and its national treasures are a testament to this world-class city.

33

Nairobi, Kenya

The Basic Facts

Nairobi is the capital of Kenya and one of Africa's most important commercial centers. Nairobi was founded on the site of a water hole called Enkare Nairobi (cold water). The city became the nation's capital in 1963 after the British granted independence to Kenya. Nairobi experienced explosive growth through the end of the 20th century and is now the largest city between Cairo and Johannesburg.

Geography

Nairobi lies at 1 degree 17 minutes south latitude and 36 degrees 49 minutes east longitude. The city is located on a high plateau beside the Rift Valley in south-central Kenya. The valley is ringed by the Ngong Hills to the west, Mount Kenya to the north and Mount Kilimanjaro to the southeast. The Nairobi River flows just north of the city center.

Climate

Nairobi is near the equator, but is more than a mile above sea level. This altitude helps moderate the city's weather throughout the year. Average temperatures are typically in the 70s Fahrenheit. The rainy seasons are spring and autumn, but annual rainfall is relatively moderate.

Government

The Kenyan government is based in Nairobi. The country is divided into eight provinces, one of which is Nairobi province. Nairobi's mayor is elected to serve a 2-year term, although provincial affairs are controlled by the national government.

Demographics

Nairobi's population is estimated at 2.5 million. Most residents are either from Kenya or other African nations that were once British colonies. Nairobi is regarded as a multi-cultural city; residents come from various African ethnic backgrounds and practice widely different religions. Regrettably, the city's crime rate has risen in recent years, largely due to the impoverished majority population. The government constantly struggles to control HIV infection and prevent AIDS-related deaths common to metropolitan areas in Africa.

Economy

Although the well-known Nairobi National Park is a popular tourist attraction, tourism does not significantly contribute to the city's economy. Manufacturing in and around Nairobi includes clothing, textiles, building materials, processed foods, beverages and cigarettes.

Railroads were a critical component of Nairobi's economic growth, and the city remains a major hub for freight and passenger traffic.

The History

Nairobi came into existence with the construction of the Mombasa to Uganda railway; the site was a convenient place for railroad workers to rest before heading into the highlands. Nairobi was established in 1899, and in 1905 became the capital of the British East Africa Protectorate. The influx of white settlers sparked friction with the local tribes, especially the Kikuyu, but these settlers helped the area to prosper through agriculture.

During the 1920s and 1930s the Kikuyu began a political movement to return the country to tribal control. One of the leaders of this movement was Johnstone Kamau, who later changed his name to Jomo Kenyatta (Swahili for Light of Kenya). He was an outspoken leader and is considered the father of the Kenyan Nation. After Kenya declared its independence from Britain—after continued international pressure—Nairobi became the nation's capital and Kenyatta became its first president.

The Sights and Sounds

Nairobi is a modern city in the midst of the African wilderness. The city is surrounded by countless species of exotic animals, and thousands of safari enthusiasts flock to the area each year. Poaching and habitat destruction over the years have contributed to a sharp increase in the number of endangered species, including the Grevy's Zebra, the northern white rhinoceros, and the African elephant. A crackdown on poaching and vigorous conservation efforts are attempting to reverse this trend.

Nairobi National Park, a 45-square-mile acre game reserve, is just outside the city.

Wild animals roam freely in their natural habitat while expert guides lead tourists on safari–although today's visitors come not to kill but to photograph.

The Giraffe Centre in nearby Karen is a park dedicated to the conservation of the Rothschild giraffe. Visitors to the 140-acre park can see the animals up close and even feed them. Giraffe Manor within the park is a luxury hotel, but do not be surprised if a giraffe suddenly pokes its head through your window! The manor was originally privately owned, but today both the Centre and the Manor are operated by the African Fund for Endangered Wildlife.

The Danish author Karen Blixen lived in Nairobi from 1913 to 1931. She wrote several novels under the pseudonym Isak Dinesen, but is best known for her memoir *Out of Africa*. Her former home in nearby Karen is now a museum that features books from her library and exhibits on her life and writing.

The vast Kenya National Museum in Nairobi houses hundreds of tribal cultural artifacts from Kenya and other African nations. Visitors can view fossil displays, human skeletons, and even footprints of Homo erectus, a predecessor of modern humans.

The David Sheldrick Wildlife Trust is a must-see. Sheldrick was a famous naturalist who fought to prevent poachers from killing elephants and other exotic African species. Sheldrick died in 1977, and today his wife operates this wildlife orphanage that houses baby elephants and rhinos. Visitors can view many of the orphaned animals and learn about efforts to reintroduce them into the wild.

The Trivia

Fact: English is the official language of Kenya, and most middle-class Kenyans speak English. The common spoken language, however, is Swahili.

Fact: Nairobi is the headquarters of the United Nations Environment Programme, which is dedicated to preserving the global environment for future generations.

Fact: The 1985 film *Out of Africa*, starring Meryl Streep and Robert Redford, is based on Karen Blixen's memoir of the same name.

Fact: The movement for Kenya independence was fueled after World War II, as returning African soldiers who had been aligned with the Allies rejected the colonial government of their homeland. The soldiers helped fuel the bloody Mau Mau Rebellion which lasted from 1952 to 1960.

Fact: In 1898, as a railway bridge over the Tsavo River was under construction, two maneless male lions attacked and killed nearly 140 railroad workers. The lions terrorized the workers' encampment for months before they were finally killed by the construction engineer. The maneaters became known as the Ghost and the Darkness, and they now reside in a display case at Chicago's Field Museum of Natural History.

Why Nairobi Is a *50 plus one* City

The sights and sounds of Nairobi may appear modest by world standards, but the city is central Africa's most populous city and continues to grow. Nairobi represents the growing awareness of Africa and its natural riches, history and culture, and the city reflects the dramatic change from colonial times to the present.

34

New York City, United States

The Basic Facts

New York City is the largest city in the United States and its metropolitan area is one of the largest in the world. In many ways the Big Apple has a tremendous influence on the U.S. and the world, so much so that nearly 40 million tourists visit the city each year. There is so much to see and do that visitors need at least a week to enjoy its remarkable sights and sounds.

Geography

New York City lies at 40 degrees 40 minutes north latitude and 73 degrees 58 minutes west longitude. The city is located in the southeast corner of New York State and comprises five counties, known as boroughs: Manhattan, Brooklyn, The Bronx, Queens and Staten Island. The Hudson River separates Brooklyn from Staten Island, and the East River separates Queens and Brooklyn from Manhattan and The Bronx. Together, the five boroughs cover over 450 square miles. The area of Manhattan is the smallest of the five, but is the most densely populated; Brooklyn has the highest population at roughly 2.5 million. The New York metropolitan area includes parts of northeastern New Jersey, southwestern Connecticut, northeastern Pennsylvania, and southern New York State.

Climate

New York City's weather changes with the seasons; winters are cold and snowy and summers are hot and humid. Average annual temperatures range from the upper 30s Fahrenheit in winter to the lower 80s Fahrenheit in summer. Spring in New York City is usually mild, making this one of the best times to visit the city.

Government

New York City's government is more centralized than most other major U.S. cities. The government is not only responsible for municipal services (e.g., fire, police and public works), also for public education, penal institutions, libraries, and recreational facilities. The mayor and the 51 city council members of the city council are elected to 4-year terms. In addition, each borough elects its own borough president to a 4-year term. Borough presidents act as mayoral advisors occasionally serving on special city committees.

Demographics

New York City is a melting pot of many cultures and ethnic groups. During the 19th and early 20th centuries, the city was the main port of entry for waves of European immigrants, many of whom remained in the area and created their own ethnic enclaves. New Yorkers hail from all parts of the world, but nearly two-thirds of them are of African, Irish, Italian, Jewish and Puerto Rican descent. The population of the city itself is more than eight million.

Economy

New York City is one of the world's most important centers of industry, trade and finance. These businesses provide nearly seven million jobs for area residents. The city is home to the headquarters of many important U.S. financial institutions. The American Stock Exchange (AMEX) is located here, as is the New York Stock Exchange (NYSE)—the largest in the U.S. and a key exchange for the world economy. Although most people consider New York an urban center, it ranks third in the nation in terms of manufacturing. Among the most important industries are printing, publishing and clothing production.

The History

Native Americans originally settled in the area that would become New York City. The English explorer Henry Hudson discovered Manhattan in 1609. The Hudson River, which now bears his name, is the river on which he sailed north to Albany. The Dutch were the first Europeans to live on Manhattan Island, and built a city that they called New Amsterdam.

In 1664 the British arrived in the harbor at New Amsterdam, conquered the city, and changed its name to the New York. The city was a frequent battleground during the early years of the Revolutionary War, and in 1785 became the temporary capital of the new United States. New York soon surpassed other major American cities such as Boston and Philadelphia in size and importance, due to its large natural harbor and an influx of European immigrants.

In 1883 the completion of the Brooklyn Bridge linked Manhattan and Brooklyn. Other communities became the boroughs of The Bronx, Queens and Staten Island, and in 1898 the newly formed New York City encompassed all five boroughs. At that time the city had more than three million residents. Many

Manhattan residents relocated to other boroughs, after other bridges and the subway began to operate; Manhattan, however, remained the most powerful of the boroughs. Several fiscal crises befell the city during the 20th century, and public strikes were common. New York City successfully endured these hardships and in the 1980s its economy began to improve.

Until 2001, the imposing twin towers of the World Trade Center (WTC) dominated the New York City skyline; they are now a bygone symbol of the city. The WTC suffered two significant terrorist attacks in its history. On February 26, 1993, a car bomb exploded below the North Tower of the World Trade Center, killing six people and injuring more than 1,000. On September 11, 2001, terrorists hijacked two commercial airliners and flew them into the North and South Towers. Both towers collapsed within hours, and more than 2,700 people lost their lives. The tragedy galvanized the city and country to carry on throughout grief and adversity. Plans have been approved to build a memorial to the victims on the site.

The Sights and Sounds

The sights and sounds of New York City are virtually endless. The city's dozens of neighborhoods each have a distinct identity, and some of their names—Chelsea, Greenwich Village, SoHo, and Little Italy, to name a few—are as famous as the city itself.

Manhattan is the center of this metropolis—the most visited and most recognized area of the city. Nothing says Midtown Manhattan quite like the Rockefeller Center and Radio City Music Hall. Named for the famous philanthropist and oil tycoon, Rockefeller Center is a massive upscale business area that covers some 22 acres of prime real estate. A plaza in the complex becomes an ice-skating rink during the winter, delighting both New Yorkers and tourists. Radio City Music Hall is the largest indoor theatre with nearly 6,000 seats, and is home to the world-famous Rockettes. Fifth Avenue is paradise for those shoppers with deep pockets. St. Patrick's Cathedral is a short distance away at the intersection of 50th Street and Fifth Avenue. This glorious Gothic church, dedicated in 1879, is the largest Roman Catholic cathedral in the U.S. The United Nations is headquartered in Manhattan along the East River.

Times Square is famous—and infamous—for its checkered past as a seedy and dangerous side of town. A major clean-up effort swept away the peep shows and adult movie theaters in favor of attractions more palatable to tourists. Its main intersection at 42nd Street and Broadway is the site for New Year's Eve celebrations, annually attracting nearly one million revelers to party in the streets. Times Square is home to Broadway, a popular spot for theatergoers interested in first-run entertainment. While many tourists appreciate that this area is now safer, cleaner, and more attractive, hard-core New Yorkers feel Times Square has lost its luster.

It is impossible to visit New York City without seeing the Empire State Building. This 102-story office building is a beautiful Art-Deco style skyscraper. When it was completed in 1931, it was the tallest building in the world. Tenants were few in the building's early years, presumably as a result of the economic collapse during the Great Depression. Today, however, the Empire State Building is the city's media center; it is the base for many commercial television and radio stations. An elevator whisks visitors to the outdoor observatory on the 86th floor, from which tourists can take in a fabulous view of the city's skyline.

The museums of New York are world-famous and world-class. The Metropolitan Museum of Art, near Central Park, is a day trip all in itself. Every notable era in art and architecture is represented here. The museum's collection is so large that exhibits must be periodically stored so others may be displayed. The representative exhibits for each period are said to be the best in the world. The Solomon R. Guggenheim Museum, designed by Frank Lloyd Wright, is the city's museum of modern art. Its continuous spiral architecture gives it a futuristic appearance–perfectly suited to the exhibits contained within. The American Museum of Natural History is the largest in the world and perhaps the most significant museum of its kind. Exhibits include everything from ancient skeletons and huge meteorites to the 563-carat Star of India sapphire.

An afternoon spent strolling Greenwich Village is an afternoon well spent. Famous for its writers and artists, it is also gracious is a funky sort of way, with quaint, tree-lined streets. The stores, shops, restaurants and the adjacent Washington Square with its famous Memorial Arch make touring an enjoyable event.

Even the most jaded New Yorker appreciates the ferry ride from Battery Park to Ellis Island, where the 152-foot tall Statue of Liberty looms over New York Harbor. From 1892 to 1954, more than 12 million immigrants were processed at the federal immigration station at Ellis Island. The island is now a national monument and museum. The Statue of Liberty was a gift from France as a gesture of friendship between the two nations. It was dedicated in 1886 to commemorate the United States centennial.

While in Lower Manhattan, take in Fraunces Tavern, best known as the site of General George Washington's farewell address to his officers. The New York Stock Exchange is nearby on Wall Street.

The Trivia

Fact: In 1653, Dutch colonists on Manhattan built a large wall along the northern edge of the town to discourage attacks. The wall was abandoned after it fell down shortly afterward. The colonists chose to build a road in its place, which became known as Wall Street.

Fact: The Erie Canal, completed in 1825, was critical to the growth of New York City's economic importance. The canal linked the city to points west and in effect led to the growth of major cities throughout the Midwest.

Fact: For more than 150 years, Tammany Hall was the name of New York City's Democratic Party machine. The group garnered the immigrant vote by offering jobs, gifts and advice to the new arrivals. William M. (Boss) Tweed was the most notorious of the group's leaders. When he was removed from power in 1872, he was imprisoned and charged with bilking the city of several million dollars.

Why New York City Is a *50 plus one* City

Love it or hate it, New York City represents the United States to the world. Crowded, aggressive, dynamic and ever-changing, the city is a symbol of capitalism, great entertainment, celebrities, enormous buildings and a style all of its own. Critics have frequently written off New York City as unworkable and unmanageable, but each time the city proves them wrong.

35

Prague, Czech Republic

The Basic Facts

Prague is the capital and largest city of the Czech Republic, and is also one of the oldest cities in central Europe. Prague was once the capital of the former Czechoslovakia, but in 1993, following the collapse of the Soviet Union, Czechoslovakia split into two independent countries: the Czech Republic and Slovakia. Prague remained the capital of the Czech Republic.

Geography

Prague lies at 50 degrees 5 minutes north latitude and 14 degrees 26 minutes east longitude. The city is located on both banks of the Vltava River in the central part of the Czech Republic. Many bridges link the two banks of the river, but the most famous is the historic Charles Bridge. Prague covers nearly 2,000 square miles. The city has been called the city of a hundred spires for its many churches.

Climate

Prague's north-central European location lends itself to a climate of extreme weather. Average temperatures range from the lower 30s Fahrenheit in winter to the mid-80s Fahrenheit in summer. Spring and autumn are normally cool and wet.

Government

Prague's main governmental body is the City Assembly, which consists of 70 elected members. The Assembly oversees municipal policies and elects the 11-member City Council. This City Council is charged with implementing city services and includes a mayor, four deputy mayors, and six councilors.

Demographics

Czechs constitute the vast majority of Prague residents. The city had a large German-born population prior to World War II, but Czechoslovakia expelled most Germans after the war. Since the latter half of the 20th century immigration to

Prague has been tightly restricted by the government. This policy, combined with a low birth rate among residents, means the city's population has only slightly increased since the end of the war. Many of the city's older buildings have remained in poor condition, a factor that has contributed to a citywide housing shortage.

Economy

Prague is one of the Czech Republic's leading manufacturing centers. Its industries produce aircraft engines, automobiles, beer, chemicals, furniture, machine tools, and processed foods. Over the last few years, many international companies have moved their headquarters to the city. Prague was relatively undamaged during World War II, and so the city has become a popular location for films that are set during or before the war.

The History

The city is believed to have been founded in the 9th century. It soon became a major trading center and eventually the residence of the Bohemian kings. Many of the city's most impressive buildings were constructed in the 14th century during the reign of King Charles IV, then ruler of the Holy Roman Empire; he saw Prague as a new Rome. Charles also founded the first university in Prague in 1348.

Prague was the home of the Hussite religious reformation in the 1400s and suffered damage from the religious wars that soon followed. The Thirty Years' War began in Prague in 1618, when Protestant Bohemians rebelled against the Roman Catholic Habsburgs. Their revolt failed, and the Habsburgs ruled the city and surrounding country until after World War I.

In 1918, Prague became the capital of the new country of Czechoslovakia. German troops occupied the city during World War II, and thousands of Czechoslovakians were killed, especially Jews. The Soviet Union then held sway over the city in support of the Czechoslovak Communist Party. In the late 1980s, Prague was a center for the movement to end Communist control of central Europe.

The Sights and Sounds

The beauty of Prague, aside from the obvious art and architecture, is that the city is reasonably compact and easy to explore. Most of historical Prague is within an hour's stroll of the Charles Bridge—and a slow-paced stroll at that, allowing visitors time to take in the sights and sounds of this wonderful, majestic city.

The New Town and Old Town districts contain much of the beauty and warmth of modern-day Prague. The Old Town Square, as a trading center and marketplace since the 10th century, remains very much active and is, in many ways, the heart and soul of the city. Tourists and locals alike enjoy the 600-year old Astronomical Clock Tower. The clock strikes hourly and includes an astronomical dial and the clockwork Walk of the Apostles and others.

The Old Town Hall overlooks the square, providing an excellent view of Prague from 200 feet. The Church of Our Lady Before Tyn dates from the 14th century, a monumental structure with a Gothic façade and twin spires.

Wenceslas Square in New Town is a broad avenue filled with shops, restaurants, clubs and hotels. The National Museum, founded in 1818, is an enormous Neo-Renaissance structure also located in New Town. In 1989 Wenceslas Square was the gathering-place for crowds protesting the oppressive Communist regime.

Prague has a long, proud Jewish history. The Gothic-style Old-New Synagogue survived World War II and is the oldest active synagogue in Europe. The Jewish Museum displays a collection of Jewish memorabilia gathered by Jews during World War II. The Pinkas Synagogue contains a moving testament to 80,000 Bohemian Jews–their names are inscribed on the nave walls.

Prague's most prominent landmark is undoubtedly the Charles Bridge. Like much of Prague, the Charles Bridge exists because of the Holy Roman Emperor Charles IV. The bridge was built in the 14th century, and some 30 statues were added 300 years later. These treasures were removed and placed indoors to protect them from pollution; replicas are in their place now. The bridge offers wondrous views of the city and appears to have different moods throughout the day–from quiet and contemplative early in the morning to festive at night.

Prague Castle reflects the city's historical greatness. The castle is perched on a hilltop where it has stood for more than 1,000 years. The real spirit of the Castle is St. Vitus Cathedral, which was completed over 600 years from 1344 to 1929. The cathedral features a variety of styles from Gothic to Art Nouveau, reflecting the prominent genres of each era. There are 22 chapels in the cathedral, of which the most famous and the most opulent is dedicated to Good King Wenceslas, the patron saint of Prague and Bohemia. Interestingly, Wenceslas was a prince, but never a king.

Two important museums are housed in the castle complex: St.George's Basilica, which contains ancient Czech art; and Sternbeck Palace, known for its fine European art collection. The castle ramparts are particularly favored for their splendid views of Prague.

Beer drinking is a great pastime in Prague. In fact, the Czech Republic is said to have the highest per capita rate of beer consumption in the world. U Fleku, dating back to 1499, is a sprawling beer hall, entertainment venue, and brewery museum. It is said that patrons consume over two million gallons of their dark lager annually.

The Trivia

Fact: In 1968, Prague was briefly the center of an anti-Communist reform movement. This period is sometimes referred to as the Prague Spring. The movement was soon crushed by Soviet tanks and forces from other nearby Communist countries.

Fact: Prague is made up of five medieval towns: Prague's Old Town, which dates to the 12th century; Lesser Town, founded in 1257; New Town; the Old Jewish Quarter; and Castle District, established in the 1330s.

Fact: In the late 16th century Prague became a center of the Renaissance. The Emperor Rudolph II selected artists, musicians, philosophers, and others to enrich Prague's cultural landscape. The associated artistic movement became known as European Mannerism.

Why Prague Is a *50 plus one* City

A trip to Eastern Europe would be incomplete without seeing the beauty and richness of Prague. The city's rich history, art, and architecture remained largely unscathed during World War II, and so tourists can still appreciate the centuries-old sights and sounds. To visit Prague is to live the good life!

36

Rio de Janeiro, Brazil

The Basic Facts

Rio de Janeiro, commonly known as Rio, is the second largest city in Brazil and is a major center for trade, economics and tourism. Although the city has problems of class disparity, overcrowding and pollution, it remains a popular South American tourist attraction.

Geography

Rio lies at 22 degrees 50 minutes south latitude and 43 degrees 20 minutes west longitude. The city is roughly 450 square miles in area, and is surrounded by some of the most spectacular scenery in the western hemisphere: green mountains to the north and west and crystal blue waters to the east. The city is famous for its white beaches and Sugar Loaf Mountain, which rises 1,325 feet from the peninsula in the bay.

Climate

Because Rio is located south of the equator, the winter and summer months are opposite from those in the northern hemisphere; winter occurs between June and August and summer occurs between December and February. Annual temperatures do not vary much, and tend to be in the low 70s Fahrenheit. Even so, because the city is at sea level, it is normally humid. Winters can be rainy and are sometimes marked by unusual spikes in temperature; these periods are referred to as veranicos or mini-summers. Spring is considered the most pleasant time of year.

Government

Brazil is divided into 26 states that are further divided into municipos (Rio is one of them). The city is governed by an elected mayor and city council. The state is led by an elected governor and legislature. Each state also elects an 81-member senate and 513-member Chamber of Deputies. The states elect three senators each and a number of deputies based on the state's population.

Demographics

Rio residents are commonly referred to as Cariocas. This moniker may have been created by Portuguese settlers using a Native American expression for white man's house. Cariocas have a mixed heritage of Native American, European or African descent. Unlike all other South American countries, Brazil's official language is Portuguese. Total population is estimated to be more than six million people.

Roman Catholicism is the dominant religion in Rio, but there are groups that practice Macumba, a mixture of Christian and African rites. Like many South American cities, Rio has a large disparity between classes. Impoverished people are segregated into slums, which are plagued with violence and drug problems.

Economy

Tourism is an important part of Rio's economy. The city is also one of Brazil's financial and commercial centers. Rio is responsible for about 10 percent of Brazil's industrial economy, and goods such as processed foods, chemicals, drugs and metals are manufactured here. The shipbuilding industry employs many residents as well. The city is a major transportation center; roads and rail lines link the city with most of the country and other South American cities.

The History

The area that is now Guanabara Bay was occupied by Tupi Indians when Portuguese explorers first arrived in 1502. In fact, present-day Brazil was a Portuguese colony even before the first explorers arrived. Rio de Janeiro was founded in 1565, and 2 years later the French, who had built a small settlement nearby, were expelled from the city. In 1720 gold and diamonds were discovered in nearby Minas Gerais, and Rio's natural harbor made it an ideal port to export riches to Portugal. The city grew rapidly as a result, and became the capital of Brazil in 1763. Brazil declared independence from Portugal in 1822 and Rio remained the capital until 1960, when it was moved to Brasília.

Over the next 100 years, coffee replaced gold as Brazil's top export. In the early 20th century the city was modernized with a redesigned port and an improved infrastructure. The population boomed during this period, with millions of people moving into the city from rural areas. Many of the poorer newcomers found no affordable housing other than Rio's slums, known as Favelas.

The Sights and Sounds

Rio is a city that delights the senses with its exotic mixture of old and new, indigenous and European, wealth and poverty. Where to begin? In the Centro or the city center, of course, the oldest part of Rio.

Think Rome is the only city famous for its aqueduct? Visitors in the know go to the Carioca Aqueduct, built in the middle of the 18th century to carry fresh water into the city. Modern technology has rendered the aqueduct obsolete, however, and today the massive, stone-arched structure carries not water but local trolley cars known as Bondes.

The National Library, completed by 1908, was one of the first institutions of its kind in all of South America. The library's collection dates to the 11th century and includes drawings, prints and manuscripts. The entire collection tops some 13 million books, from rare to contemporary.

While most of Rio's churches date their history and design to colonial times, one stands as an exception to the rule. The Cathedral of St. Sebastian, completed in 1976, is a massive pyramidal concrete structure that can accommodate 20,000 parishioners! Keeping in style with its ultramodern look, the altar is a simple but enormous rock of granite. The leaded windows are said to be some of the best in South America.

Rio has many churches much older than St. Sebastian: the Convent of St. Anthony, completed in 1780; the Church of St. Francis, completed in 1737; and São Bento Monastery, completed in the 1580s. All are stunning in their majesty and each deserves a visit.

Rio's museums offer a tremendous range of exhibits, and in the case of one—the Museum of the Small Farm of the Sky—a fascinating name. This museum's 20th century European collection is outstanding, with paintings by Degas, Matisse, Picasso, Dalí, and Matisse, among many others. Also here is a collection of historical maps. The National History Museum documents Brazil's lengthy colonial and national history. The museum building itself is historic; its battlements date from 1603. The National Museum of Fine Arts specializes in Brazilian works from the 19th and 20th centuries. The Museum of Modern Art showcases some 1,700 works are displayed in a contemporary building.

The Paço Imperial is the palace built in 1743 for the Portuguese viceroys, the king's colonial administrators. After Brazil declared its independence, the palace became home to the country's first emperors. Today it is a cultural center. The plaza in front of the building was once the site where emperors were crowned and deposed, and also where slavery was abolished.

Visitors flock to two particular sites for marvelous views of the city and surrounding countryside. The first, Pão-de-Açúcar, also known as Sugarloaf Mountain, is a 1,300-foot-tall granite monolith. Glass-paneled cable cars transport visitors to the peak every half hour. Corcovado is another granite mountain, world-famous for the 125-foot-tall statue at its peak named Christ the Redeemer. The statue was dedicated in 1931 and is dramatically illuminated at night. Visitors can reach the summit of Corcovado by train or taxi.

Cafes, restaurants, dance clubs and theatres are active 7 nights a week. Do not forget to visit Rio's wildly popular beaches; expect only to sunbathe, however, as pollution has made the water unsafe for swimmers. Nevertheless, the beach is the place to see and be seen.

The Trivia

Fact: Rio was the only city in the Americas to be an European capital–however briefly. In 1808, Prince John of Portugal fled Lisbon to escape a French invasion and moved the Portuguese capital to Rio. Thousands of wealthy Portuguese followed him and remained in Brazil. Lisbon again became the Portuguese capital when John returned in 1821.

Fact: When the Portuguese explorer Gaspar de Lemos discovered Guanabara Bay in January 1502, he believed it to be the mouth of a major river, which it is not. He called the bay Rio de Janeiro, which is Portuguese for River of January.

Fact: Cariocas crowd the beaches of Rio each New Years' to holding candlelit Macumba ceremonies.

Why Rio Is a *50 plus one* City

While Rio is a city of great contrasts, it has a style and appeal all its own. The city blends all of the best of Native American, Portuguese and African cultures into a festive mix of music, art and food.

37

Rome, Italy

The Basic Facts

Rome is the capital of Italy and one of the most historically significant cities in the world. Following the fall of the Roman Empire, its importance faded, but returned during the Renaissance and then grew rapidly during the late 20th century. Today millions of visitors flock to Rome each year to explore the history and experience the culture of what was once the center of the known world.

Geography

Rome lies at 41 degrees 52 minutes north latitude and 12 degrees 37 minutes east longitude. The ancient city was founded in west-central Italy along the Tiber River, about 10 miles west of the Tyrrhenian Sea. Rome's geography and its distance from the sea made it less conducive to attacks by invaders and pirates. The modern city of Rome covers roughly 500 square miles. Vatican City, a sovereign state just 0.17 square miles in size, lies within the city limits. The Vatican is the administrative and spiritual center of the Roman Catholic Church.

Climate

Rome has a mild Mediterranean climate influenced by the colder Alpine climate to the north and the hot and dry climate to the south. Average temperatures are fairly consistent throughout the year; winters average in the mid-50s Fahrenheit and summers average in the mid-80s Fahrenheit.

Government

Rome is governed by a City Council consisting of 80 members, each of whom is elected to a 4-year term. The City Council in turn elects one member from the body to be the city's mayor. The mayor heads the City Executive Committee, which is responsible for administering city services.

Demographics

Rome is homogenous in terms of its language and religion, but diverse in terms of its culture, economics and politics. Most Romans are native Italians; northern African and non-Italian Europeans make up the minority. Rome's population of 2.7 million is large by European standards, and the entire metropolitan area population is more than four million.

Economy

Commerce and government dominate Rome's economic landscape; other important industries are tourism and construction. Rome's few factories produce clothing, textiles, processed foods and other products. Many motion picture studios are located in Rome; this beautiful and historic city provides an excellent backdrop for mainstream and independent films.

The History

The first known settlers of Rome, the Latins, established a settlement along the Tiber in the 9th century B.C. Two hundred years later, the Etruscans gained political control of the region. They held power until Rome became a republic in 509 B.C.

The Roman Republic expanded its sphere of influence throughout the ensuing years; by 275 B.C., Rome controlled most of Italy. The Republic defeated the Carthaginians of North Africa during the Punic Wars in the 3rd century B.C., thereby assuming power over most of the Mediterranean region. Despite its military successes abroad, internal struggles plagued the city; economic disparity and political skirmishes led to revolt and war among the cities. Eventually, Roman general Lucius Sulla became dictator over the city and restored order.

Rome expanded further overseas under Pompey and Julius Caesar. Caesar returned in triumph to Rome after conquering Gaul, yet the Roman Senate ordered him to relinquish power. His refusal led to a civil war, and when he emerged victorious, he became dictator for life. He was assassinated in 44 B.C. by an angry group of Roman senators, an event which touched off another round of civil wars. Caesar's adopted son and heir, Augustus, became the first Roman Emperor in 27 B.C. Rome under his reign experienced a notable period of peace and prosperity, which became known as Pax Romana (Roman Peace).

After Augustus's death, a succession of rulers furthered the transfer of power from the Senate to the emperor; over time they achieved virtually absolute power. Over the next 2 centuries the Roman Empire went into decline, so much so that in 293 A.D., the emperor Diocletian divided the Empire into eastern and western regions.

The Greek city-state of Byzantium was declared the eastern capital, while Rome remained the capital of the western region. In 410 Rome was sacked by invading Barbarians, which caused the abrupt end of the Western Roman Empire.

Although Rome no longer held political power, its culture and form of government survived and helped shape much of Western civilization. During the middle ages, the Roman Catholic Church became the unifying force of Europe and modeled its administrative structure on the Roman Empire. The history of Rome was more closely examined during the Renaissance and by the 1700s books about ancient Rome began to appear.

The Sights and Sounds

Rome is a city with so many great sights and sounds, not just the Vatican or historic sites such as the Roman Forum. Visitors can wander throughout the city and find exceptional smaller, everyday sights that are as much as 2,500 years old; few cities can make this claim!

The historical center of Rome, containing those buildings that represent ancient Rome, is significant not only to Rome and Italy, but also to the entire western world. The Arch of Constantine is one of the finest examples of 4th century architecture still in existence. The Arch and Christianity go hand in hand, as Constantine first permitted the practice of the new religion.

Considering the massive size of the elaborate Coliseum, it is difficult to believe that it was built in just 8 years, from 72 to 80 A.D. With seats for 50,000 spectators, this oval-shaped stadium was the principal site for games and spectacles, including gladiatorial combat. The statue of Nero, once adjacent to the Coliseum, is believed to have been the source for its name. The arena was abandoned in 524, after the rise of Christianity sparked outrage that combatants were killed during the games staged there. Over the years, the Coliseum was damaged by several earthquakes and ransacked for its prized travertine stone. Nevertheless, this ancient structure remains one of the world's most magnificent ruins, and today serves as a rallying point for protests against the death penalty.

Nero, the Roman Emperor from 54 to 68 A.D., is famous for his excessively cruel nature; he is believed to have played his violin when Rome burned during the great fire of 64 A.D. Many historians have concluded that Nero himself ordered the destruction so that he might build the Golden House, his famous palace. More than half of its 300 rooms have been excavated; the massive, opulent building leaves both historians and tourists in awe.

Unfortunately for visitors, the Roman Forum is a shadow of its former self. The ruins of palaces, temples and civic buildings are indeed impressive, yet they provide only a glimpse into its former glory. When in Rome, the Pantheon is another must-see. Built in 27 B.C. as a temple, and later consecrated as a Christian church, this globe-shaped building is a classic example of architectural perfection.

Rome's fountains and squares, known as piazzas, are as famous as any of the city's landmarks. Traditionally, visitors to Rome ensure their return by tossing a coin into the Trevi Fountain, built in the mid-1700s. The Piazza Barberini contains the famous Triton Fountain and the Fountain of the Bees. The Piazzo del Popolo is one of the largest in Rome, famous for its ancient Egyptian obelisk. Piazza di Spagna is home to the young and the chic, who meet at the famous Spanish Steps, a 200-year old staircase named after the nearby 19th century Spanish Embassy.

Sant'Angelo Castle was built as a tomb and memorial to the great Emperor Hadrian; this fortress helped the city to defend itself against Barbarian invasions. The castle was associated with the Vatican, and many popes sought refuge there during troubled times.

Words fail to describe the treasures of the Vatican museums. The entire complex has some five miles of displays; to see everything, visitors must be both patient and dedicated. Periods represented include ancient Egyptian, early Roman and Greek, and the Renaissance masters. The painted ceiling of the Sistine Chapel, Michelangelo's greatest legacy to the world, was commissioned by Pope Julius II in 1508 and took the renowned painter 4 years to complete.

St. Peter's Square was redesigned by Bernini in the 17th century to enable large numbers of devout Catholics to receive papal blessings. St. Peter's Basilica at the square was constructed in the 16th and 17th centuries in tribute to God's greatness. The basilica's famous dome was designed by Michelangelo and is accessible by a spiral staircase. From the top of the dome, visitors can take in a lovely view of the church's intricate interior space.

After a strenuous tour of this magnificent city, tourists need to relax and enjoy life. Like every major European city, Rome has a variety of restaurants, cafes, clubs, bars and entertainment spots to suit every taste. The sights and sounds change frequently, but never fail to delight.

The Trivia

Fact: Christianity entered Rome in the 2nd century A.D. The Roman rulers were frightened of this new religious movement and brutally repressed its followers, blaming them in part for Rome's decline. Christianity thrived, however, and in 313 Constantine declared Christianity the official religion of Rome.

Fact: The head of the household in ancient Rome was called the Paterfamilias (father of the family). He had absolute power over the household and could sell his children into slavery or even have them killed. A son could not own property as long as his father lived, and so many Roman households included married sons and their families.

Fact: Ancient Romans loved spectacle. The Roman Coliseum was known for its violent games, in which trained gladiators fought wild animals–and sometimes each other–often to the death. Condemned criminals and early Christians were frequently killed for sport. On occasion, the Coliseum was even flooded in order to stage mock naval battles.

Fact: The Circus Maximus hosted chariot races in its large oval arena; today it is a park.

Fact: None of the 300 rooms in Nero's Golden House was a bedroom; the palace was built solely for his entertainment.

Fact: Many historians blame lead poisoning for the eventual decline and fall of the Roman Empire. Most Roman plates and cups were made of lead, and they frequently used lead to sweeten their wine.

Fact: Ancient Romans were proud of their physical fitness and hygiene. Emperors built lavish public baths to encourage the citizens to exercise and bathe. These baths became popular meeting places.

Why Rome Is a *50 plus one* City

Throw a coin into the Trevi Fountain and return to experience Rome's beauty all over again. The city's art, architecture and cuisine span the centuries providing visitors one of the world's finest vacation experiences.

38

San Francisco, United States

The Basic Facts

San Francisco is one of California's largest cities and is a popular tourist destination. Main attractions include Chinatown, the famous cable cars, its steep hills, and its mild climate. It is often known as the City by the Bay.

Geography

San Francisco lies at 37 degrees 45 minutes north latitude and 122 degrees 26 minutes west longitude. The city sits on the northern tip of a peninsula in northern California between San Francisco Bay and the Pacific Ocean. A one-mile-wide strait connects the bay to the ocean and was once named the Golden Gate. San Francisco occupies 121 square miles and is dominated by more than 40 hills; some hills rise as high as 400 feet, and so they have some of the steepest streets in the world. There are several islands in the ocean and bay, including the famous island of Alcatraz. The Port of San Francisco borders the bay and is one of the world's largest natural harbors.

Climate

San Francisco's rapid growth is partly attributed to its climate; annual temperatures range from the mid-50s Fahrenheit in winter to the upper 60s Fahrenheit in the summer. San Francisco experiences significant fogs over the western part of the city, especially at night and in the early morning; warm air flows over the cold ocean waters to form this meteorological phenomenon.

Government

San Francisco has been a consolidated city-county since 1856; the mayor is also the county executive. The city is run both by the mayor and an 11-member city council called the Board of Supervisors. The mayor appoints the heads of city government services and prepares an annual budget. The mayor has veto power over laws and regulations passed by the Board of Supervisors.

Demographics

Caucasians comprise nearly half of the population of San Francisco; significant minority groups include Asians, African-Americans, and Native Americans. San Francisco has the largest Chinese population in the United States, and the city's Chinatown is the largest in the country. Many Chinese immigrated to work in gold mines and on the Central Pacific Railroad. The city's population is estimated at 744,000, but that of the metropolitan area is more than 7.5 million.

Economy

San Francisco is a leading U.S. financial center as well as a commercial and industrial center. Tourism is vital to the economy, and many San Franciscans work in the tourist trade. The city is at the heart of California's burgeoning high-tech industry; the area from Palo Alto to San Jose is commonly known as Silicon Valley.

The History

In 1769 Spanish explorer Gaspar de Portolà discovered the area surrounding present-day San Francisco. A few years later, the Spanish built a military fort in the area and established a nearby mission. Mexico declared independence from Spain in 1810 and took control of California for the purpose of cattle ranching. The resulting trade in cattle hides led to the development of a busy port at San Francisco Bay.

In 1847 the United States acquired San Francisco following the Mexican-American War. The port area boomed during the Gold Rush of 1849, and San Francisco was incorporated as a city in 1850. Lawlessness prevailed in the late 1800s, despite the efforts of citizens to curb the trend.

In 1906, the massive San Francisco earthquake killed at least 3,000 people and destroyed nearly the entire city; the resolute citizens quickly rebuilt the area. The expansion of ports in Los Angeles and Oakland lessened the importance of San Francisco's port. The city underwent a major makeover in the 1960s; older dilapidated buildings were replaced by modern row houses. The population became more diverse as the building boom continued through the 1970s.

The Sights and Sounds

The federal penitentiary Alcatraz, known as The Rock in its heyday, was built in 1934 on Alcatraz Island in the middle of San Francisco Bay. Some of the United States' most dangerous criminals were imprisoned there, including the notorious gangster Al Capone. By 1963, however, the prison was closed because it became too expensive to maintain. Today it is a National Historic Landmark, and guided tours are available through the building and around the grounds. The West Coast's oldest lighthouse still in operation is also located on Alcatraz Island.

The collection at the Asian Art Museum spans a period of 6,000 years. Works include art from many Asian countries housed in 30 galleries. Because the space is so large, take the time to look at the special exhibits before you try to browse the whole collection.

The Japanese Trade and Cultural Center, a local area known as Japantown, is organized around the Peace Pagoda. This group of five buildings houses Japanese restaurants, museums, art galleries, bookstores and cultural attractions. Each year, the Kabuki Theatre hosts the Asian American Film Festival.

Golden Gate Park, with its beautiful hills and turquoise waters, is the perfect destination for hikers, bikers and picnickers. The park is a welcome break from the bustle of the city. Noteworthy sites here are the Japanese tea garden, the Victorian-styled Conservatory of Flowers greenhouse, and the Strybing Arboretum and Botanical Gardens.

Built in 1937, the Golden Gate Bridge was once the world's largest suspension bridge. It is the undisputed symbol of San Francisco and a popular tourist attraction. To see the fog rolling in at the bridge is a wonderful treat for tourists.

The collections at the Palace of the Legion of Honor range from ancient artifacts to European paintings and ceramics. The museum is known for its extensive collection of sketches, paintings, and sculptures by Auguste Rodin.

A visit to San Francisco is not complete without a trip to Chinatown; more than 10,000 people live in this neighborhood. Shops cater both to tourists and locals. Take a detour from the main streets and wander the alleys and side streets, and follow your nose to some wonderful Chinese food at reasonable prices.

At Fisherman's Wharf, make sure to visit the sea lions at Pier 39; you will hear them before you see them! Board the ferry to Alcatraz Island here. The San Francisco Maritime National Historic Park is located nearby; explore the maritime museum and tour the turn of the century ships at Hyde Park Pier. This is also a great location for lunch or dinner, with something for everyone; pricy restaurants with bayside views, sidewalk bars, and snack shops. People-watching is a popular activity here as well.

Sonoma Valley, the home of many of California's best vineyards, is a short drive from San Francisco. If you have an extra day, visit the wineries of Sonoma; many offer guided tours and gift shops. The surrounding countryside, with its rolling hills, is a beautiful and relaxing change from the city.

Muir Woods National Park, just 12 miles north of the Golden Gate Bridge, is the home of California's giant redwoods. These towering trees can grow to more than 350 feet and have a life span of well over 600 years.

The Trivia

Fact: Lombard Street in San Francisco is the crookedest street in the world. It is on a hill so steep that the street would be impassible otherwise. There are eight turns, or switchbacks, in one city block.

Fact: San Francisco was closely identified with the counterculture of the 1960s. The Haight-Ashbury area was a major center of the hippie movement. Many well-known musical talents emerged from the scene, including the Grateful Dead and the Jefferson Airplane.

Fact: In October 1989, San Francisco experienced the Loma Prieta earthquake. Although fatalities were few in comparison to the 1906 quake, costs to repair the resulting structural damage were in the billions of dollars. The quake is also known as the World Series quake; it struck before Game 3 of the 1989 Bay Series between the San Francisco Giants and the Oakland Athletics.

Fact: In 1978, Mayor George Moscone and Supervisor Harvey Milk (the first openly gay man ever elected to public office in the United States) were shot and killed by Dan White, a disgruntled and troubled city supervisor. White was convicted of involuntary manslaughter, but committed suicide soon after his release from prison.

Fact: The Spanish army post of the Presidio covers over 1,500 acres in northwestern San Francisco. It was the headquarters of the U.S. 6th Army until 1995, and is now operated by the National Park Service. The Presidio Officers' Club, built in 1776, is the oldest building in the city.

Why San Francisco Is a *50 plus one* City

Even the locals leave their hearts in San Francisco. The city is vibrant and metropolitan, with wonderful weather and a great standard of living. The districts within the city invite exploration and discovery, with fine restaurants and ethnic cuisine. The city has a reputation for tolerance, quality employment and unfortunately, exorbitant real estate prices. Once you are there, you cannot afford to leave–for many reasons!

39

Seattle, United States

The Basic Facts

Seattle is the largest city in the state of Washington and is a manufacturing, trade, and transportation center. The city is a popular tourist destination for shopping, dining, and recreation.

Geography

Seattle lies at 47 degrees 36 minutes north latitude and 122 degrees 20 minutes west longitude. The city is located on the eastern shore of Puget Sound, an arm of the Pacific Ocean. Puget Sound is linked to the Pacific Ocean by the Strait of Juan de Fuca. Seattle covers 84 square miles and its downtown area extends eastward from Elliott Bay, an inlet of Puget Sound. The downtown area is surrounded by so much water, including Lake Washington and Union Bay, that it often seems like an island. The actual metropolitan area of Seattle includes King, Snohomish and Island counties. Seattle is framed by the Cascade Mountains to the east and the Olympic Mountains to the west. Mount Rainier, an active volcano, is part of the Cascades and is clearly visible from the city.

Climate

Seattle is known for its wet weather and temperate climate. Temperatures average in the mid-40s Fahrenheit during the winter and mid-60s Fahrenheit during the summer. Although many believe Seattle is a rainy city, there are cities on the East Coast that have a higher annual average rainfall. Seattle's precipitation tends to be more misty than rainy, and when it is not raining, it is usually overcast.

Government

Seattle's has a mayor-council form of government; the mayor and nine city council members are elected to 4-year terms. All city offices are non-partisan.

Demographics

Almost three-quarters of Seattle's population is Caucasian; most are of German, Irish, English or Scandinavian descent. Asians and African-Americans are the two next largest ethnic groups. The city's population is more than 580,000, while the population of the metropolitan area is roughly 3.8 million.

Economy

Service, manufacturing, and shipping industries are vital to Seattle's economy. Health care, government and the military are the primary employers in the service industry. Manufacturing centers around aircraft, software, and computer supplies. Although the Boeing Company is the region's largest employer, as of 2001 its headquarters are now in Chicago. The software giant Microsoft and the video-game maker Nintendo are headquartered in Seattle.

The History

The area was inhabited by Indian tribes long before it was first settled in 1852 by pioneers from Illinois led by Arthur A. Denny. Their settlement was Alki Point, a beach on Puget Sound. The first sawmill in the area opened the next year, and Seattle became a shipping center for lumber from Washington's forests.

Seattle grew rapidly after rail lines were established in the late 19th century, although in 1889 most of Seattle business districts were destroyed by fire. The city recovered, however, and experienced another growth spurt during the Alaskan and Klondike Gold Rushes soon afterward. The area's economy began to diversify in the early 20th century with the growth of agriculture and the fishing industry. Seattle became important to the war effort during World War I, and manufactured ships, aircraft, and related products. The defense industry grew further during World War II and the population surged as a result. After a series of ups and downs in the defense industry in the late 20th century, Seattle reinvented itself as a tourist destination.

The Sights and Sounds

Nestled between the Cascade Mountains and Elliott Bay in Puget Sound, Seattle is a metropolitan center with heart. Famous for coffee and grunge rock, this city is known for its laid-back charm and fabulous seafood. The interesting mixture of arts, technology and scenery make Seattle a must-see for outdoor enthusiasts and art lovers.

No visit to Seattle is complete without a trip to the Space Needle, a structure originally built for the 1962 World's Fair. The tower is 605 feet tall, has an observation deck near the top, and a restaurant called Sky City which rotates to give patrons a 360-degree view of the city. The Space Needle is part of the Seattle Center, which includes the Center House, the Pacific Science Center, and two movie theaters.

Pioneer Square is an historic district that is now home to trendy restaurants, antique bookstores and jazz clubs. This location is also rumored to be the hub of Seattle's nightlife. You can wander around, explore the old buildings and peek in at the shops, or visit a trendy restaurant or hot spot.

Pike Place Market is one of the major tourist attractions in Seattle. Built in 1907 and covering an area of nine acres, the market is filled with hundreds of shops, flower markets and restaurants. The original Starbucks store is here, along with dozens of other interesting shops. The open-air setting and the clientele make this a huge people-watching destination. Be sure to take in the flying fish at the Pike Place Fish Market; onlookers delight in watching fishmongers throw fish to one another.

The Experience Music Project is an eclectic museum which was funded by Paul Allen of Microsoft. There are hundreds of interactivie exhibits as well as a gift shop, restaurant and bar. Visitors can play musical instruments and even make their own recordings. The collection also includes rock-and-roll memorabilia from such icons as the Beatles, Jimi Hendrix and Bob Dylan. If visitors need any other enticements, the museum was designed by the avant-garde architect Frank Gehry.

The Museum of Flight has an extensive collection of aircraft and flight simulators. There are exhibits on famous pilots, what they wore, and what they carried in combat. The flight simulators alone are worth the price of admission.

Most visitors recognize Seattle as the home of Starbucks coffee. The city has a lively coffee culture with many local coffee shops vying for top honors with the big guys. Locals recommend Zeitgeist Coffee for its up-and-coming art, and the excellent java near Pioneer Square. Other hometown heroes include Café Ladro and Vivace. While Starbucks and Seattle's Best on the corner are popular, real java junkies swear by the artistic expression of their local baristas.

Mount Rainier National Park is a few hours southeast of Seattle and is well worth the trip. The views of the coast and the mountains are beautiful, and the hiking trails are first-rate.

The Trivia

Fact: After the disastrous 1889 fire leveled much of Seattle, the city engineers raised the level of the downtown streets several feet above sea level. Doing so left many intact storefronts below street level. The Seattle Underground Tour in Pioneer Square visits this hidden realm.

Fact: The economic boom of World War I led to the rise of powerful labor unions in Seattle. After the war, the unions were afraid they would lose power due to the need for fewer defense workers. In February 1919, 60,000 union workers staged a 5-day strike to voice their concerns. It was the nation's first general strike and was called the Seattle Revolution of 1919.

Fact: Tourism in Seattle was given a major boost when the city hosted the World's Fair in 1962. The fairgrounds are now called the Seattle Center (including the famous Space Needle) and they, and the monorail that was built at the same time, are major tourist attractions.

Fact: The Nisqually Earthquake struck Seattle in 2001, causing injuries and significant property damage but no fatalities.

Fact: Seattle has been on the forefront of several cultural movements. The most famous (and most contrasting) is the birth of the Northwest School of Painters in the 1930s and 1940s and the creation of grunge rock in the 1990s.

Fact: Seattle is home to 25 theatre companies. The only U.S. cities with more theatres are New York City and Chicago.

Why Seattle Is a *50 plus one* City

Seattle is environmentally beautiful, virtually surrounded by water and mountains; few can resist its magnificent setting. In addition, the city is clean, safe, culturally alive, and simply an inviting and invigorating place to live and visit.

40

Shanghai, China

The Basics

Shanghai is the largest city in China, the country's largest port, and a world center of finance, trade and industry. Shanghai experienced a building boom in the late 20th century, as thousands of new buildings and a new subway system were added. The new development included the Pudong Area, on the east side of the Huangpu River, as an international financial center.

Geography

Shanghai lies at 31 degrees 14 minutes north latitude and 121 degrees 27 minutes east longitude. The city is located on the Huangpu River in the eastern part of China. The Huangpu and Yangtze Rivers meet and empty into the South China Sea only 14 miles north of Shanghai. This location helped establish Shanghai as China's leading port.

The city of Shanghai actually lies within the Shanghai Municipality, which is divided into three areas: the old foreign section in the north, the original Chinese settlement in the south and the suburban areas that surround both sections. Some rural counties and offshore islands are also included in the municipality.

Climate

Shanghai has a moderate climate in the winter with temperatures averaging in the 40s Fahrenheit. Summers can be warm and humid with temperatures averaging in the high 80s and low 90s Fahrenheit. Rainfall is prevalent, especially in the spring. Winters can be gray and dreary with some snow. Shanghai is also affected by periodic typhoons, which are the Pacific Ocean's equivalent of hurricanes.

Government

The Shanghai Municipality is divided in 18 districts and one county. The municipality is ruled directly by the national government.

Demographics

Few Shanghai residents are descended from the original inhabitants of the old walled city. Nearly all registered residents of Shanghai are descended from 19th and 20th century immigrants from the adjacent provinces of Jiangsu and Zhejiang. This sense of local identity has been diluted in recent years as people from other Chinese regions have moved here. Language differences and other social problems have generated ill will among those who consider themselves authentic Shanghainese. The population of greater Shanghai is estimated at a staggering 17 million.

Economy

Shanghai is China's leading port and one of its most important industrial areas. Major manufacturing industries include machinery, ships, cement, electrical equipment, textiles, and furniture. Shanghai also has a strong agricultural base; suburban farmers raise cereal grains, vegetables, pigs and fish. In recent years, the communications industry has gained in economic importance.

The History

The city of Shanghai began in 1553, which is rather late in comparison to other major Chinese cities. However, there is evidence that it was a trading center as early as 960. Because the city was not considered a major center until the 19th century, there are few ancient artifacts or historical buildings.

The city was a small trading center before 1842, when the British opened the area to international trade at the end of the Opium War. Other Western nations quickly followed Britain into Shanghai, yet foreign influence came under fire in the early 20th century by Shanghai citizens.

The Japanese captured Shanghai in 1937 and occupied the area until the end of World War II. In 1949, in the wake of the communist rise to power in Shanghai, most foreign companies left the city for Hong Kong.

The Chinese communist government enlarged Shanghai and expanded its industrial base. In the 1960s, Chairman Mao attempted to purge the country of his enemies during the Chinese Cultural Revolution, and the student-supported Red Guards drove the government from the city. After a brief period of military control, Shanghai returned to civilian control in 1979.

The Sights and Sounds

Shanghai is a cosmopolitan city with two sides. The old foreign city, (called Pu Xi or West City) includes colonial buildings, while the Chinese City across the river (called Pu Dong or East City) includes modern skyscrapers. Both the old and new Shanghai are visible in almost every block. At night, the city seems to glow from the lights atop the newer buildings.

The Bund (Zhongshan Road) is in the old foreign side of the city; colonial buildings in every architectural style cover the main thoroughfare. At night, visitors can see the lights on the skyscrapers across the river in the Chinese City. A boat cruise down the river at night includes beautiful sights and scenery on both sides.

An old racecourse, the People's Square is now an open-air park in the middle of the city. Surrounded on all sides by buildings, the park is a wonderful green space in the middle of a busy metropolis. Trees, gardens and benches make this a good place to take a much-needed break from the action.

The Shanghai Museum is near to the People's Square. Reputed to be the best museum in all of China, this structure is four stories tall with thousands of artifacts in its collection. Each gallery is huge and full of explanatory placards in both Chinese and English. The museum is so large and the collection so extensive that visitors can spend several days trying to see everything.

Jade Buddha Temple is one of the most important Buddhist temples in China. The temple's exterior is not architecturally significant, but the large statue of the sitting Buddha inside the temple is well worth a visit. This statue is made of white jade and weighs more than a ton.

Nanjing Lu Street is Shanghai in a microcosm. Visitors can walk from the People's Square down this street to the Bund. All along the way, tourists and locals mingle in a mélange of shops, restaurants, snack bars and businesses. At night, the gleam of neon makes this street the Chinese version of Times Square.

The soaring Pearl Tower is a symbol of the new Shanghai to locals. The tower is a huge tourist attraction with a restaurant and museum. There can be long lines on the weekends, so go early. The views of the city are marvelous and especially beautiful at sunset and as the lights go on at night.

The Trivia

Fact: During the pre-World War II years, Shanghai became synonymous with exploitation and vice. The city featured opium dens, gambling halls and brothels. These areas were actually guarded by the Western nationals who occupied the city.

Fact: After the British opened the city to international trade, the city created special areas, or concessions, in order to segregate foreign nationals from the rest of the population.

Fact: China's Communist Party was founded in Shanghai in 1921. The creation of the party caused a major conflict with the emerging Chinese Nationalist Party, which would eventually gain brief control of the country. During this early conflict, the Chinese Nationalists prevailed in the city, killed many Chinese Communists, and drove others from the city.

Fact: Westerners may be surprised by the crowds of children who beg from tourists. Visitors who want to be left alone should not give money to anyone who begs. Tourists who hand out even small coins will be followed all across the city.

Why Shanghai Is a *50 plus one* City

The explosive growth and dynamism of this city attracts people from throughout China and the world. While very young compared to many Chinese cities, Shanghai has attracted world attention for its bustling streets and its modern ways–mixed, of course, with the old.

Singapore

The Basic Facts

Singapore is an independent city-state, a bustling center of finance, trade and manufacturing. During the late 20th century, Singapore grew into one of the most stable and populous nations in Asia.

Geography

Singapore lies at 1 degree 18 minutes north latitude and 103 degrees 52 minutes east longitude. It is located at the southernmost tip of the Malay Peninsula where the South China Sea and Indian Sea converge. Singapore consists of one large island, covering 221 square miles, and over 50 smaller islands covering another 18 square miles. The large island, also called Singapore, contains the capital and houses most residents.

Singapore is built around the harbor with warehouses and docks lining the port. The city is roughly divided between the commercial section and the Jurong area, an industrial park west of the city.

Climate

Singapore's temperature is consistent throughout the year with highs averaging about 80 degrees Fahrenheit. Thanks to cool sea breezes, the temperature rarely rises above 95 degrees Fahrenheit. The climate, however, is rainy; Singapore annually receives about 95 inches of rain. The rainiest months are during the monsoon season, from November to March. June to October is the driest period of the year.

Government

The city-state of Singapore is ruled by a democratic government. Members of the Unicameral Parliament are elected to 5-year terms. The prime minister and cabinet administer government functions.

Demographics

Singapore is one of the world's most densely populated areas. Chinese constitute three-quarters of the population, Malays constitute 15 percent and Indians make up the remainder. Singapore has no official religion. Various ethnic groups practice Buddhism, Islam, Christianity, Taoism and Hinduism, among others.

Economy

Prior to the 1960s, Singapore's economy was based on trade. Its economy has become more varied of late and now includes the financial and transportation industries. Singapore's annual per-capita income is one of the highest in Asia, and it has a low rate of unemployment. Singapore is a major manufacturing center, producing chemicals, electrical and electronic equipment, machinery, rubber, plastics, and other goods. Tourism is an important part of Singapore's economy; some eight million tourists visit every year.

Cars overcrowd the city, so much so that drivers have to pay a fee to enter during peak traffic periods. Singapore's mass-transit system has helped alleviate some of the traffic congestion. Singapore is linked to nearby Malaysia via a bridge and causeway, but most visitors arrive through Changi International Airport, located on the eastern end of the large island.

The History

It is believed the Singapore islands were a small trading center when the Chinese arrived in the area in the 1300s. In 1390, a Sumatran prince named Parameswara took over the area. Ten years later the city became known as Shingapura and later Singapore.

The Portuguese occupied the city in 1511 and eventually destroyed most of it in 1613. Trade emerged in the early 1800s when Sir Thomas Stamford Raffles of the British East India Company arrived and established a trading colony to offset the Dutch influence in the region. The new port was a huge success, and shipping facilities were enlarged in the 1850s.

The opening of the Suez Canal in 1869 was a boon for Singapore, which exported Malaysian tin and rubber. Mass immigration led to lawlessness, however, until the early 20th century. During the Great Depression in the 1930s, Singapore deported many immigrants to their home countries.

Although Singapore was heavily fortified by the British, the Japanese invaded and conquered the area in World War II. After the war, the British regained control of Singapore for a short time before an independence movement emerged in the city. Singapore declared independence from Britain in 1963 and the government allied itself with nearby Malaysia. The relationship between the two countries was tenuous, however, and they dissolved their partnership after just two years.

The Sights and Sounds

The north bank of the Singapore River was originally the seat of colonial government for the island. This area is now known as the Historical District, where the British and others built most of the government buildings. The Asian Civilizations Museum, located in the Empress Place Building, is said to be one of the best museums in Singapore. First opened in 2003, the museum houses an excellent collection of art, artifacts, jewelry and relics from the various cultures represented in Singapore. The Empress Place Building was originally constructed by the British to run the colonial government.

The Padang in downtown Singapore is a large open field where the British and other Europeans participated in sports and outdoor ceremonies. During World War II the Japanese used the field as a holding pen for British and other non-Asian residents. The area is surrounded with the symbols of colonialism and government, including City Hall, Parliament House, and the Cricket Club.

The Raffles Hotel, named after Sir Stamford Raffles, was built in 1887 to accommodate the upper classes that were making their fortunes in Singapore. The Raffles Hotel symbolizes Singapore's boom-and-bust history. In the 1920s it was the place to be; its famous dining room and ballroom were all the rage. But the Great Depression, World War II, and stiff competition from newer hotels nearly bankrupted the grand dame. In the 1980s the hotel was restored to its original beauty and gained prominence again in the city. Its Long Bar is still the place for the movers and shakers of Singapore society.

The Chinatown Heritage Centre keeps alive the history of the ethnic Chinese in Singapore. Three shops in this enclave have been restored to give visitors a glimpse into life in old Chinatown. The displays include antiques from the time of immigration and re-creations of shops, houses and public buildings.

The religious traditions of Singapore are a fascinating mix of East and West. The Armenian Church dates back to 1836 and services are still held there–but not by its own members. St. Andrews Cathedral, rebuilt in the 1850s, is the oldest Anglican church in Singapore, although its old English Gothic style may look somewhat out of place in this Asian setting. Other notable religious structures include Nagore Durgha Shrine, dedicated to a Muslim holy man who visited Singapore spreading the message of Islam; Sri Mariamman Hindu Temple, the oldest Hindu temple in Singapore; Thian Hock Keng Temple (the temple of heavenly bliss), the city's oldest Chinese temple; Wak Hai Cheng Bio Temple, also

Chinese; and Sri Veerama Kaliamman Temple, a Hindu temple dedicated to the goddess Kali.

Singapore has delightful parks and reserves, among them Tiger Balm Gardens, Jurong Bird Park (with a collection of some 8,000 birds) and the Singapore Botanic Gardens. Most visitors take a trip to Sentosa Island either by monorail or by ferry from the World Trade Center on the main island. Sentosa is an oft-visited island resort with lovely beaches and luxury hotels. Its attractions include the 360-foot-tall Carlsberg Sky Tower, Underwater World, the Musical Fountain, and Fort Siloso.

Night life in Singapore centers on two areas called Boat Quay, which once was a notorious opium den, and Clarke Quay, which was a former industrial site. Both have the nightlife, cafes, restaurants, bars and clubs that visitors enjoy late into the night.

The Trivia

Fact: The original name of Shingapura is a puzzle. The name means lion city, but lions are not native to Singapore. The actual name might have been Singapura which is connected to Buddhism (Buddha was often symbolized by a lion in ancient Indian art).

Fact: As part of his plan for modern Singapore, Sir Thomas Raffles divided the city into distinct enclaves known as kampongs; immigrants were segregated according to their ethnic groups. In many respects, these divisions exist to this day.

Fact: In the early 19th century Singapore was plagued by pirates who plundered exports from departing ships. This problem continued into the 1850s and beyond, despite the efforts of local merchants and British colonialists to stem the raids.

Fact: Between 1825 and 1873, India used Singapore as a penal colony. Many of the Indians who later settled in the area were convicts sent to Singapore to work as laborers.

Fact: Many locals speak Singlish, a hodge-podge regional dialect with English, Chinese, and Malay roots.

Why Singapore Is a *50 plus one* City

Visitors to this remarkable city will understand its significance in the pantheon of the world's greatest cities. Modern, prosperous and multicultural, Singapore stands among the economic giants of Asia. The city is safe and clean, and visitors are invited to explore and enjoy the sights and sounds without any concern.

St. Petersburg, Russia

The Basic Facts

St. Petersburg is the second largest city in Russia. It is a major port and the former capital of the country. The city is one of the largest industrial and cultural centers in the world. The city takes its name from the Russian czar Peter the Great who founded the city in 1703.

Geography

St. Petersburg lies at 59 degrees 57 minutes north latitude and 30 degrees 20 minutes east longitude. The city is located in northwestern Russia at the eastern end of the Gulf of Finland (an arm of the Baltic Sea). Peter the Great wanted to create the city in the style of Western European cities, and so its design mimics that of cities such as London, Paris and Vienna.

St. Petersburg lies on a marshy lowland where the Neva River flows into the Gulf of Finland. The city center is located on the southern bank of the Neva.

Climate

St. Petersburg's climate is generally damp and rainy, thanks to its location near the Baltic Sea. Winters are cold with temperatures averaging in the 20s Fahrenheit. Summers are cool with average temperatures in the upper 60s Fahrenheit. In winter daylight is minimal, because the city is so far north of the equator. Conversely, during the summer months twilight lasts all night, giving rise to the white nights for which the city is famous.

Government

St. Petersburg is divided into 18 city districts; the city itself is the capital of a provincial area known as the Leningrad Oblast. The governor controls city government, territorial and industrial branches, and administrative boards.

Demographics

City residents are primarily of Russian heritage, from a variety of ethnic groups. In an attempt to curb the recent rapid population increase, the government has instituted a strict policy: potential residents must either have a job and residence or marry an existing resident. Despite this restriction, a large number of undocumented residents have contributed to the city's congestion. The population is estimated to be 4.5 million.

Economy

Shipbuilding has been an important industry since the city was founded. During the Industrial Revolution the city emerged as an important manufacturer of machine tools; this manufacturing segment comprises nearly 40 percent of the city's industry. Other industries include chemicals, electrical equipment, textiles, nuclear equipment and timber. St. Petersburg has an excellent port and railroad network, and so is a major national trade and distribution center.

The History

Peter the Great intended to make St. Petersburg the first Western city in Russia, and he hired Western architects to design its layout. The city soon became the intellectual and social center of Russia, and it grew rapidly during the 18th century. In the late 19th and early 20th centuries, several popular movements against czarist rule were centered here.

The Russian Revolution toppled the czarist government of Nicholas II and enabled the Bolsheviks to seize power; their leader V.I. Lenin became head of their new government. The capital was moved back to Moscow in 1918 as Lenin fled from potential foreign invasion. Lenin died in 1924, and St. Petersburg—which had been known as Petrograd since 1914—was renamed Leningrad in his honor.

Leningrad was the site of one of the most famous battles of World War II, when the German army laid siege to the city for almost 3 years. Even though more than a million Soviets perished—mostly from starvation—the city did not fall to the Germans. After World War II, many of the city's historic structures were rebuilt, and the government began a massive campaign to build new housing. As Communist control of the Soviet Union waned in the late 1980s, non-Communists assumed control of Leningrad's government. A failed coup attempt in Leningrad by Communist hard-liners in 1991 spurred the Soviet Union's final collapse, and in that same year, the city's official name reverted to the original St. Petersburg.

During the Communist regime, many of St. Petersburg's classic buildings fell into disrepair through neglect. Restoration is now underway, due largely to the fact that Russia's current leader, Vladimir Putin, was born and raised in the city. In 2003,

St. Petersburg celebrated its 300th anniversary.

The Sights and Sounds

Palace Square and the adjoining Winter Palace certainly are St. Petersburg's most famous landmarks of the city. The Italian architect Bartolomeo Rastrelli designed the sprawling structure–all 1,057 rooms–as well as many of the adjoining buildings. The palace is now part of the State Hermitage Museum, with a collection so vast that visitors are often overwhelmed by the sheer number of exhibits. Of particular import are the Egyptian collection and the works of the Italianate masters and the Impressionists. The 155-foot-tall Alexander Column, built as a tribute to Emperor Alexander I, features prominently in the center of Palace Square.

The Peter and Paul Fortress, located on an island in the Neva River, was the original military stronghold of the city. Until 1917, its prison housed political prisoners including Dostoyevsky, Trotsky, and Peter the Great's own son, Alexei. Peter and Paul Cathedral, with its needle-thin spire and rich baroque style, dominates the center of the fortress. The church is the burial site of nearly all Russia's former emperors and empresses. The remains of Nicholas II and his family were reburied there in 1998, after having been recovered from an ignominious grave after the fall of Communism.

In the center of St. Isaac's Square is its namesake, the magnificent St. Isaac's Cathedral. This church, built in the 19th century, is in the Neoclassical style and has a striking golden dome. Its ornate interior includes granite and marble fixtures, paintings, and mosaics. Until 1917 this was the main cathedral of the Russian Orthodox Church. The monument to Nicholas I on the square is unique among equestrian statutes, in that it has only two support points: the legs of his horse.

Decembrists Square is named for the revolutionaries of 1825 who rebelled against Russia's autocratic government, The Bronze Horseman, an imposing monument to Peter the Great, is a short distance away and faces the Neva River; its pedestal resembles a wave and reflects Russia's then merging sea power.

Arts Square is named for the series of museums and concert halls in the area, including: the Russian Museum, the world's largest museum of Russian art, with over 400,000 works; the Ethnography Museum, which represents all the ethnic cultures of the former Soviet Union; the St. Petersburg Philharmonic; and the Maly Theatre for opera and ballet. A statue of the Russian poet Pushkin stands in the middle of Arts Square.

The Church of Our Savior on the Spilled Blood is built on the site at which Czar Alexander II was mortally wounded by a dissenter—this in spite of his openness to Russian reform. The church was intentionally modeled after St. Basil's Cathedral in Moscow's Red Square.

The palace and park of Petergof (Peter's Court) is a jewel of St. Petersburg. It is nicknamed the Russian Versailles for its series of parks, palaces, and fountains. The palace, which originally served as an exquisite summer residence for the Russian czars, is now a museum surrounded by masterful landscaping.

The Trivia

Fact: This beautiful and grand city was built on a mosquito-ridden swamp using thousands of Swedish prisoners of war as slave labor.

Fact: Czar Nicholas II, who would later be deposed and killed by Bolshevik revolutionaries, authorized his troops to kill hundreds of unarmed demonstrators in 1905 in front of the Winter Palace. This event came to be known as Bloody Sunday and spurred the revolution of 1905.

Fact: St. Petersburg was designed in the 19th century by a commission including the noted Italian architect Carlo Rossi. Empress Elizabeth carefully reviewed and refined the commission's plans, and Catherine the Great extended the designs into the Neoclassical genre.

Fact: St. Petersburg has played a pivotal role in Russian literature and is the setting for works by Alexander Pushkin, Fyodor Dostoyevsky and Andre Bely.

Fact: St Petersburg's nearly 500 bridges gives the city's its nickname, the Venice of the North.

Fact: The entire city of St. Petersburg has 140 museums that display more than three million art objects.

Why St. Petersburg Is a *50 plus one* City

Imagine the sheer tenacity to build a beautiful city in a swamp and build it with the finest minds in art and architecture of the day—and have it survive for 300 years through every sort of political and social upheaval. Not even wars and massive destruction could destroy St. Petersburg. Not only does the city survive, but it thrives, with it culture and art being restored after years of neglect. Visitors are awed by the city, its museums and its culture.

Stockholm, Sweden

The Basic Facts

Stockholm is the capital of Sweden and is the country's largest city. Gentrification efforts in the 20th century replaced entire sections of the city with modern architecture; Stockholm continues to renew itself today.

Geography

Stockholm lies at 59 degrees 23 minutes north latitude and 18 degrees east longitude. Stockholm is located on the east coast of Sweden, between Lake Mälaren and the Baltic Sea, on the mainland and 14 islands. The city is connected by 53 bridges. Thousands of other islands are located near Stockholm and are a recreational haven for city residents.

Climate

Stockholm's weather is normally cool and temperate, and precipitation is moderate throughout the year. The summers are mild and usually sunny, with average temperatures in the upper 60s and lower 70s Fahrenheit. Winters are dark, cold and snowy, with average temperatures in the lower 30s Fahrenheit.

Government

The city and its environs comprise the Stockholm Municipality, an administrative region that is further subdivided into 18 district councils or boroughs. Each borough is responsible for its own elementary education, social services, and leisure and cultural services. Stockholm County's responsibilities include healthcare, public transportation, and various cultural institutions.

Demographics

Stockholm's population, like most of Sweden, consists mainly of Scandinavians of Germanic descent. In recent decades immigration has led to a sharp rise in the city's population and ethnic diversity. Many immigrants, most of whom are from the neighboring countries of Finland, Norway, and Denmark, come to the city as guest workers. Some recent immigrants have fled the conflicts in the former Yugoslavia. The population of the city itself is roughly 1.2 million.

Economy

Stockholm is the center of Sweden's economy and government. Most city residents are employed in the service industry and more than 30 percent are employed in local or national government. Insurance, commerce and banking are important to the city's economy, as is manufacturing, which includes publishing, chemicals, machinery, and metal products.

The History

The name Stockholm first appears in the Chronicle of Eric, thought to be written between 1322 and 1332. According to the chronicle, the city was founded by Birger Jarl, who built a castle in the area now known as Gamla stan. Stockholm became a major trading center because goods being transported between the lake and the sea had to be transported by land through the city. The iron trade was particularly important to the city of Stockholm and the surrounding area. During Stockholm's early years, the city was vastly overcrowded and suffered from frequent destructive fires.

In 1523, Gustav Vasa became the first king of Sweden, and led a rebellion against Denmark, which at the time controlled most of the country. Sweden's independence had a major impact on Stockholm, and the city moved further toward economic and political importance.

Stockholm became the capital of the Swedish empire in 1634. Trading regulations gave the city a monopoly on trade with foreign merchants. Also during this period, prosperous city residents built palaces and large castles, and immigration to the city increased dramatically.

By the beginning of the 18th century, Sweden's and Stockholm's influence had begun to wane. The Black Death struck the city in 1713, and several areas of the city were destroyed in 1721. Stockholm revived, however, and in the 19th century acquired a reputation as a European cultural center–a reputation that continues to this day. New hospitals, post offices, and transportation systems helped to modernize the city, and its economy thrived due to increased trade and commerce.

The Sights and Sounds

Stockholm's great sights are located in a relatively compact area, mainly in Gamla stan. This is the old city, also known as the town between the bridges. This part of the city is on an island south of the city center and is known for its streets and squares that date to medieval times. The earliest inhabitants of this area were German, and the house designs and architecture reflect their cultural influences. The large square in the middle of the district, known as Stortorget, was the site of the Stockholm Massacre in 1520, when the Swedish nobles and clergy were slaughtered by Danish forces under King Christian II. This event prompted Sweden's move toward eventual independence.

The Royal Palace is the official residence of the Swedish monarchy, although the royal family resides at Drottningholm Palace outside Stockholm. In the 13th century Birger Jarl built a fortress on this site to defend against foreign naval invasion. The fort was converted to a palace in the late 16th century, and rebuilt a century later in the Baroque style. Tourists and locals enjoy the ceremonial changing of the guard outside the palace, which takes place each day at noon.

The Stockholm City Hall, completed in 1923, is an unusual and imposing building. The famous Blue Hall (which is not blue at all) is the site of the annual Nobel Prize banquet. The building's 348-foot tower dominates the area.

Stockholm has many world-class museums. The Museum of Modern Art, which opened in 1998, features some of the finest works of both regional and international artists. The National Museum's collection focuses on the Old Masters, while the exhibits at the Nordic Museum display folk art, costumes, and artifacts from Sweden's 500-year history. The Skansen is an open-air museum that includes traditional buildings that have been rebuilt, as well as a zoo, an aquarium, and an amusement park. The Vasa Museum displays the only surviving 17th century ship, the Vasa; this is the most popular and most-visited museum in all of Scandinavia. The collection of 19th century carriages at the Royal Stables in Stockholm is the finest collection in the world; among the most famous is the Seven-Glass Coach. Visitors must take guided tours to see the museum's treasures.

For the best view of Stockholm, visitors flock to the Kaknastornet, a television tower owned by the National Swedish Broadcasting Company, Teracom. The 508-foot-tall tower has both indoor and outdoor observation decks that allow for impressive views of the city.

The Trivia

Fact: The fires that plagued Stockholm during the 14th century were a benefit to the city. Newer, safer buildings retained the medieval charm of the old structures.

Fact: Stockholm features nearly 70 performing arts venues, 60 museums, and various art galleries. It is the home of Sweden's Royal Ballet and Stockholm University.

Fact: Residential suburbs were built in the 1950s and 1960s on land that was purchased in the early 20th century for future redevelopment; this is but one example of Stockholm's reputation for far-sighted city planning.

Fact: There are more restaurants per person in Stockholm than in any other European capital. The traditional lunch buffet is the big meal of the day and is an enjoyable occasion.

Why Stockholm Is a *50 plus one* City

Stockholm is one of the cultural capitals of Europe, as well as an important trade and commercial center. The city's blend of culture, architecture, natural beauty, and charm makes it a popular destination for international tourists. If nothing else, visitors enjoy the city based on its sheer physical beauty, its cleanliness, and its sense of order.

Sydney, Australia

The Basic Facts

Sydney is the oldest and largest city in Australia and is also the capital of New South Wales. It is an important industrial city and has a major international port.

Geography

Sydney lies at 33 degrees 55 minutes south latitude and 151 degrees 17 minutes east longitude. Sydney lies on a large natural harbor known as Port Jackson, which is commonly called Sydney Harbour. Sydney and its suburbs cover nearly 500 square miles in southeast Australia. Downtown Sydney occupies the south side of Sydney Harbour and the oldest section of the city lies near the waterfront. Sydney has suburbs to the north and south. Ku-Ring-Gal Chase National Park is north of the city and is famous for its Aboriginal rock paintings and carvings.

Climate

Sydney's climate is consistently mild throughout the year, with moderate precipitation. Winter temperatures average in the mid-60s Fahrenheit, and summer temperatures average in the upper 70s Fahrenheit. Because Sydney is located south of the equator, the winter and summer months are opposite from those in the northern hemisphere; winter occurs between June and August and summer occurs between December and February.

Government

The metropolitan area of Sydney lacks an overall governing body, but is managed by local government areas; the state government of New South Wales designates duties to these areas. The city itself is run by an elected Lord Mayor of Sydney and a council.

Demographics

Most Sydney residents, known colloquially as Sydneysiders, are Australian-born of British descent. Many of their ancestors came to Australia either as settlers or as convicts (New South Wales was originally a British penal colony). Sydney's population includes Italian, Greek, and Asian immigrants, and a small number of Aborigines, those native to Australia. The population of Sydney's metropolitan area is more than 4.2 million.

Economy

Sydney is a major manufacturing center for Australia; its industries produce machinery, chemicals, paper goods, and food products. The city is also a major international livestock and wool market, thanks to the expansive cattle and sheep ranches in the outback. Sydney is also Australia's business and financial hub.

The History

Aborigines are believed to have inhabited the area for perhaps 40,000 years. Captain James Cook of Britain first visited the Sydney region in 1770, and by 1788 the British had established a penal colony there. A smallpox epidemic swept through the native population in 1789; by 1820 only a few hundred Aborigines remained in the area

The area became troubled by conflict, not only with Aboriginal tribes, but also between landowners and freed convicts. Sydney was incorporated in 1842, and in 1850 the British penal colonies were closed.

The city boomed during the late 1850s, thanks in part to the discovery of gold in the nearby town of Bathurst. The city population grew rapidly during the 20th century, especially after World War II, and Sydney became a sprawling urban center with the usual problems that plague fast-growing cities: overcrowding, pollution, and traffic congestion.

Many historic buildings were demolished in the mid-20th century to make way for modern skyscrapers. Various districts sprung up to reflect the city's many ethnic groups. Sydney hosted the 2000 Summer Olympics.

The Sights and Sounds

This is a hip and happening city. Sydney has something for everyone: white-sand beaches, warm ocean waters, beautiful mountains, and a captivating cityscape. Whatever you like to do on vacation, you can find it in Sydney.

Critics and locals despised the Sydney Opera House when it opened in 1973, but today this striking building is the city's most-recognized landmark. For a small fee, visitors can tour the interior, but those short on cash can enjoy the fabulous view of Sydney Harbor from the Opera House.

The Royal Botanic Garden, near the Opera House, is home to over 7,500 species of plants. The location is a restful spot for people-watching or for a picnic lunch under the shade trees. A train shuttles patrons around the facility.

The Rocks is the oldest conclave in Sydney, with fine restaurants and trendy local art galleries. Although the area has been recently renovated, its old-world charm remains in the buildings and streets. The Rocks' tourist center offers both guided and self-guided walking tours at reasonable rates.

Darling Harbor offers further people-watching opportunities. This popular tourist attraction includes a maritime museum, aquarium, the Chinese garden, and an IMAX theater. Major shopping attractions are also here, of course, as well as a variety of family-friendly restaurants.

The Queen Victoria Building is a shopper's dream. This center, known as the QVB, is an indoor mall containing dozens of shops and restaurants in a Byzantine architectural setting.

Fox Studios is a family-friendly location that includes theaters, an ice rink, and an operating movie studio (the recent motion picture *Moulin Rouge* was filmed here). Visitors can tour the movie-making factory and enjoy interesting interactive exhibits on makeup and cartooning.

Hyde Park is an expansive outdoor park with many statues and memorials. Two notable memorials are the Anzac War Memorial honoring Australia's dead in WWI, and Lady Macquaire's Chair, a memorial to the wife of Governor Lachlan Macquaire, the park's designer. This vantage point provides an excellent view of Sydney Harbour.

Sydney boasts a number of white-sand beaches beside beautiful turquoise waters. Two of the best known are Bondi and Manly Beaches; everyone from families with children to serious surfers and beach bunnies come to soak up the sun. Visitors who choose not to sunbathe may stroll the two-mile Beach Walk from Coogee Beach to Bondi Beach; the views from the Walk are beautiful, and there are plenty of places to rest as well at nearby shops and restaurants.

Cricket and rugby are popular Australian sports, but the Aussies are mad for footy. This unique brand of football is played on an oval field that may be as much as 200 yards long, and the players' uniforms resemble those worn in rugby (i.e., without any padding). Take in a game if you have time.

The Trivia

Fact: During the early part of World War II, four Japanese midget submarines were discovered in Sydney Harbour and were sunk. Shortly thereafter, the Japanese mother submarine shelled the waterfront suburbs of Bondi and Rose Bay; many panicked residents left the city for the nearby Blue Mountains.

Fact: The city was named by the first governor, Arthur Phillip, in honor of British nobleman Thomas Townshend, the Viscount Sydney.

Fact: The government, troubled by the loss of many historic buildings during the boom of the 20th century, restored many historic buildings in the oldest section of the city, known as the Rocks. The area is now a major tourist center.

Fact: Sydney is sometimes referred to as the gateway to Australia, because most international tourists enter the country through Sydney's Kingsford Smith International Airport.

Why Sydney Is a *50 plus one* City

Sydney is a friendly, vibrant city that invites visitors to enjoy its hospitality and warmth. A visit to the Sydney Opera House makes the trip to the city worthwhile in its own right–whether you are an opera buff or not.

Tokyo, Japan

The Basic Facts

Tokyo is the capital of Japan and one of the world's largest and most modern cities. It is the seat of Japan's government and is a center of business, culture and education. Tokyo was largely destroyed by bombing in World War II; after the war, Tokyo was rebuilt and the economy and the population boomed.

Geography

Tokyo lies at 35 degrees 42 minutes north latitude and 139 degrees 46 minutes east longitude. The Tokyo urban area includes the manufacturing cities of Chiba and Kawasaki. The city is on the southeastern coast of Honshu, the largest island in Japan, and is located in the southern part of the Kanto Plain. It is bordered by the Edo River to the northeast, Tokyo Bay to the east, and the Tama River to the south. The Sumida River flows through the eastern part of the city and empties into Tokyo Bay. Mount Fuji, Japan's highest and most famous mountain, is about 60 miles southwest of Tokyo.

Tokyo is divided into 23 wards. The land on the city's far eastern side was reclaimed from Tokyo Bay, and thus is prone to seasonal flooding.

Climate

The climate in Tokyo, and all Japan for that matter, varies widely due to its location in the Pacific Ocean. Summers are generally hot and humid and winters are typically dry. Average temperatures range from the upper 40s Fahrenheit in the winter to the upper 80s Fahrenheit in summer. On clear days, Mount Fuji is clearly visible and often appears to float in the clouds.

Government

Tokyo's official name is Tokyo Prefecture. This area consists of the city, or ward area; 25 suburban areas west of the ward area; several towns in a mountainous western area; and the Izu and Bonin Islands. The governor heads the Tokyo

Metropolitan Prefecture and is publicly elected to a 4-year term. The legislative body is the 127-member Metropolitan Assembly, all of whom are elected to 4-year terms. In addition to the central government, each ward, suburb, town, or village in the Prefecture has a form of local government with an elected council, mayor, or other administrator. Their power is limited by the prefecture.

Demographics

Tokyo's population density is among the highest in the world at 33,000 people per square mile. More than 12.5 million people live in the city itself, while more than 36.5 million live in the Greater Tokyo Area. Tokyo's population is overwhelmingly Japanese, with small concentrations of Chinese, Koreans, Filipinos, Americans, and Britons.

Economy

Tokyo is a world center of economic activity and traditionally was the heart of the Japanese manufacturing industry. Goods manufactured in Tokyo include chemicals, food, electronics, furniture and paper. In the late 20th century, service industries such as communication, finance and trade supplanted manufacturing as the most important part of Tokyo's economy. Many of the world's largest electronic firms, such as Hitachi, Toshiba, Sony and NEC are headquartered in Tokyo.

Tokyo Bay is rather shallow for a successful port, so most imports and exports pass through nearby Yokohama. Tokyo has an extensive public transportation system of rail lines and buses, yet an increasing number of residents drive cars and cause significant traffic congestion. High-speed shinkansen, or bullet trains, link Tokyo to Osaka and other Japanese cities. The city's two major airports are Tokyo International, or Haneda, and Narita International.

The History

In 1457 a warrior named Ota Dokan built a castle there to take advantage of the site's strategic military location; the town of Edo formed around the castle. In 1590, a warrior named Tokugawa Ieyasu made Edo his headquarters when he became shogun, the military ruler of Japan. Edo became the nation's political center, but Kyoto remained the official capital of Japan because it was there that the emperor resided.

Tokyo and Japan voluntarily isolated themselves from the Western world in the early 17th century. In 1853 the United States naval officer Commodore Matthew C. Perry sailed into Tokyo Harbor to negotiated trade agreements with the Japanese rulers.

Emperor Meiji (also known as Mutsuhito) seized control of Japan in 1867, moved the capital to Edo, and renamed it Tokyo. A powerful earthquake destroyed much of the city in 1923; the subsequent reconstruction increased the westernization of the city that had begun in the 19th century. Tokyo was devastated by the United States during World War II bombing raids, and many buildings were destroyed. After the war, skyscrapers and other modern buildings were constructed in the city, and strict building codes were implemented to prevent future earthquake-related damage. Tokyo's population tripled between 1945 and 1960; this rapid growth, combined with insufficient city planning, led to housing shortages and traffic congestion. Tokyo improved its air and water quality in the 1990s, but overcrowding and skyrocketing property values continue to be a problem.

The Sights and Sounds

Tokyo is a crowded, bustling city, but its crime rate is low, enabling visitors to feel safe even in the wee hours of the morning. Many sights and sounds are familiar to Westerners, but still more are traditionally Japanese. Many people take time from work to admire the cherry blossoms in April.

The Tokyo National Museum, housed in eight buildings, exhibits an unmatched collection of Asian antiquities including paintings, sculpture, archaeology, calligraphy and decorative arts. The National Museum of Modern Art showcases the works of modern Japanese artists in three buildings: the Art Museum, the Crafts Gallery, and the National Film Center. Visitors may need a whole day to explore just one of these buildings.

The Kabuki-za Theater, located in the Ginza, was built especially for Kabuki performances, which include traditional Japanese music, dance and theater. Most Kabuki performances are several hours long, but the theater offers a shorter performance in the morning. Visitors may also watch from the fourth floor and leave when they wish without disturbing other theatergoers.

Ginza is the high-end shopping district in the city with many department stores, boutiques, designer outlets and trendy restaurants. This district never seems to sleep; the sidewalks are crowded both day and night. The neon signs in the Ginza District rival Times Square in their brightness and variety. If you are looking for electronics, Akihabara is the place to go. The latest techno-gadgets are on display in hundreds of shops that specialize in all types of electronic devices.

The Ryogoku Kokugikan is the heart of sumo wrestling in Tokyo; three annual tournaments are held here. The attached Sumo Museum displays woodblock prints, ceremonial garb, and other historical items related to this popular sport. Local restaurants offer a hotpot dish called chanko-nabe, the staple diet of sumo wrestlers. Training facilities, called stables, are located near the stadium, and some stables allow visitors to watch practice sessions.

The Meiji Shrine is a Shinto temple dedicated to Emperor Meiji and his wife Empress Shoken. Located amidst beautiful tree-lined grounds, this shrine is a good place to rest and relax without battling the crowds. Tours of the buildings are available. The Zojo-ji Temple is a Buddhist temple located in Shiba and is surrounded by a public park. The Sangedatsu Gate at the entrance to the temple was the only structure on the site that survived World War II. Six members of the Tokugawa shogunate are buried here.

Two of the finest Japanese gardens in Tokyo are Koishikawa Korakuen and Rikugien. Koshikawa Korakuen was built during the time of the Tokugawa shogunate and displays landscapes of China and Japan in miniature. Rikugien (or six poems garden) recreates scenes from 88 famous Japanese poems in a network of pools, islands, and teahouses. Both gardens charge a nominal entrance fee.

The Trivia

Fact: Tokyo means eastern capital in Japanese.

Fact: Tokyo was spared by the atomic bombs that the United States dropped on Japan in 1945; bombing raids earlier that year had already destroyed at least one-third of the city and killed hundreds of thousands of residents.

Fact: The Imperial Palace in Tokyo is the home of the Japanese emperor. It consists of several buildings connected by beautiful landscaped grounds. The palace buildings and inner grounds are only open to the public on January 2nd and the emperor's birthday, December 23rd.

Fact: Shinto and Buddhism are the major religions of Tokyo, and many shrines and temples are available for worshippers and visitors.

Fact: Tokyo's subways and commuter trains are so crowded during rush hours that oshiya (literally pushers) are employed to shove commuters into the packed trains.

Why Tokyo Is a *50 plus one* City

Tokyo's traditions and its prominence in the global economy make it a great city. The sheer beauty of Mount Fuji, ever-present against the cityscape, awes visitors from around the world. Visitors and locals alike cherish the city for its excitement, history and power. Tokyo is a modern metropolis, crowded and clamorous, yet also artistic and culturally aware.

Toronto, Canada

The Basic Facts

Toronto is the largest city in Canada and the capital of the province of Ontario. It is a principal center for the nation's manufacturing, financial, and communications industries.

Geography

Toronto lies at 43 degrees 40 minutes north latitude and 79 degrees 23 minutes west longitude. The city occupies 243 square miles on the northwest shore of Lake Ontario, and the metropolitan area of Greater Toronto covers more than 2,700 square miles. Three rivers travel south through the city and empty into Lake Ontario: the Humber, the Don, and the Rouge.

Climate

Toronto has a fairly mild climate relative to the rest of Canada, thanks to Lake Ontario's moderating effect. Temperatures range from the 30s Fahrenheit in winter to the 70s Fahrenheit in summer. Autumn and spring days can be spectacular with clear and cool weather. Winter temperatures occasionally drop below freezing, and the area typically has one or two major snowstorms every winter.

Government

Toronto was once composed of six locally-controlled metropolitan areas. In 1997, however, the Ontario Provincial Legislature merged these six entities to create the city of Toronto. This unified city is run by a single government and is directed by the Toronto City Council. The council, which consists of a mayor and 44 council members, is responsible for nearly all city services and operates a variety of municipal agencies, boards, and commissions.

Demographics

Toronto's population is among the world's most ethnically diverse; more than 100 languages are spoken by some 150 ethnic groups. Toronto experienced significant population growth during the mid-20th century with an influx of European immigrants, primarily from Italy and Portugal. The city's population is roughly 2.5 million and the Greater Toronto Area has more than five million residents.

Economy

Toronto is the major industrial center for the nation. Chief industries include food processing, printing and publishing, and paper, rubber and wood manufacturing. Toronto is also the country's banking and financial center, and is the home of the Toronto Stock Exchange.

The History

The area's first inhabitants were Algonquin and Iroquois Indians, who portaged across the site between Lake Huron and Lake Ontario. In the mid-18th century, French explorers built a trading post and began to colonize the area. During the French and Indian War, the French burned Fort Rouillé (later Fort Toronto) to prevent it from falling to the British. Britain won the war, and in 1763 the French ceded most of their Canadian territory in the Treaty of Paris.

John Graves Simcoe established a permanent settlement on the site in 1793 and replaced Newark as the capital of Upper Canada. He named the settlement Fort York in honor of the Duke of York. York was later renamed Toronto and received its city charter in 1834. The rise of transportation and the manufacturing industry caused the city to grow rapidly in the late 1800s. Toronto became a major market for grain and livestock once the Canadian government opened new areas in the west.

Toronto's industrial economy expanded during both World Wars due to the demand for war materials; European immigration rose as a result. To help the area meet the demands for these new immigrants, the Ontario legislature in 1954 created the Municipality of Metropolitan Toronto, a federation of Toronto and 12 of its suburbs. In 1967, the legislature merged the 13 units into six. Toronto underwent significant urban renewal in the late 1960s with the creation of improved transportation systems, housing and shopping areas. To avoid duplication of services, the Ontario legislature merged the six municipalities into the unified city of Toronto in 1997.

The Sights and Sounds

Toronto is a metropolitan center with a comfortable small town feel. While it offers everything a visitor could want in a city center such as art, theater, museums, fine dining and the like, it also offers quirky attractions such as the Bata Shoe Museum and bohemian areas like the old Distillery District. With its low crime rate, Toronto may well be the safest big city in North America.

The shopping mecca of Eaton Centre is one of Toronto's main tourist attractions. The mall contains more than 500 shops and restaurants, as well as a movie theater and a police station. Eaton Centre is the model of a successful indoor mall; visitors can find nearly everything they wish to buy. This is a fine place to wander out of the elements in winter when bitter winds blow.

Hockey is to Canadians as baseball is to Americans: it is the national pastime, and fans are loyal to their favorite teams. The Hockey Hall of Fame is located in downtown Toronto and is a must-see for fans of this fast-paced sport. Attractions include the historical hockey jerseys, plaques dedicated to former players and broadcasters, interactive exhibits popular with children, and a gift shop. The showcase of the museum is a vault–literally a former bank vault–within which the Stanley Cup and other National Hockey League trophies are displayed.

Bata Shoe Museum, located near the University of Toronto, is a museum that presents the history of footwear. Among the collection's 10,000 pairs of shoes are those of Elton John, Madonna, Michael Jordan, Picasso, and even a sock worn by Napoleon.Three of the 50 tallest buildings in the world are located in Toronto: First Canadian Place (72 stories); Scotia Plaza (68 stories); and TD Canada Trust Tower (53 stories). All three offer good views of the city and many camera-worthy angles.

Harbourfront Centre has interesting shops and restaurants, and offers plenty of people-watching opportunities. Local artists and artisans practice their crafts here, including glass blowing and jewelry making. Many small art galleries and cafes are also within this complex, which is on the waterfront south of the city center. Other attractions include an IMAX theater, musicals, and dance productions.

Toronto Island Park is divided into three sections: Centre Island, Ward's Island and Hanlon's Point. Centre Island includes a children's playground called Centreville with rides appropriate for little people. This section also includes a hedge maze, lots of green space, and plenty of room for children to explore. Both Ward's Island and Hanlon's Point are quieter spaces with more green space and no rides. Families can bike, rollerblade, walk or picnic in all three sections, and the local ferry stops at each.

Old Fort York was destroyed during the War of 1812–by Canadians, who ignited the city's gunpowder supply and blew up the fort. The structure was later rebuilt, and today it houses the world's finest collection of buildings from that area as well as exhibits on the war's history.

Tourists flock to Casa Loma, a majestic 98-room castle north of the city. This structure, built for the financier Sir Henry Pellatt, has secret passageways, hidden doors and beautiful period decorations. The five-acre gardens are also well-designed and lovely almost any time of the year.

The Royal Ontario Museum–also known as the ROM–houses a collection of over five million pieces. Its most interesting exhibit is the display of Chinese art and artifacts. The facility is currently undergoing renovation, which will create a dramatic new entranceway and new gallery spaces.

Niagara Falls is 2 hours away by car, and this is a great side trip if you have time. There are observation areas on both the U.S. and Canadian sides, but the latter has a better view of the famous Horseshoe Falls. Among the most popular attractions here is the Maid of the Mist boat ride, which takes tourists almost to the very base of the falls; the rushing water creates a deafening roar.

The Trivia

Fact: The CN Tower, at 1815 feet tall, is the world's tallest free-standing tower. Television and radio transmissions, including those of the Canadian Broadcasting Corporation (CBC), emanate from the tower.

Fact: U.S. troops captured Toronto during the War of 1812 and burned parts of the town including the fort. The troops looted the town and took the Mace, the ceremonial staff used by the legislature. President Franklin D. Roosevelt ordered the Mace returned in 1934.

Fact: Many Canadians were unhappy with British rule during the 19th century. In 1837, William Lyon Mackenzie led a revolt in the Toronto area, but the protest was quickly crushed by British troops. Mackenzie later became the first mayor of Toronto.

Fact: Toronto's film industry has experienced a tremendous boom, as its labor costs are much lower than those of United States studios. The city frequently doubles for cities such as New York and Chicago. Casa Loma appears prominently in the first X-Men film as the School for Gifted Mutants.

Why Toronto Is a *50 plus one* City

Toronto is beautiful, sophisticated, and one of the safest cities in the world. This global city prides itself on its cosmopolitan atmosphere and sophisticated urban environment, a view that is not lost on the countless tourists who visit each year.

47

Vancouver, Canada

The Basic Facts

Vancouver is the largest city in British Columbia and the busiest port in Canada. The growth of trade between Canada and Japan in the late 20th century made Vancouver's seaport even more important. The city became a modern metropolis as a construction boom continued into the 1990s. Vancouver will host the Winter Olympics in 2010.

Geography

Vancouver lies at 49 degrees 16 minutes north latitude and 123 degrees 6 minutes west longitude. The city is located in southwestern British Columbia, approximately 25 miles north of the U.S.-Canadian border. The port is in the natural harbor of Burrard Inlet; the Strait of Juan de Fuca to the south is the main water route to the Pacific Ocean.

Climate

The protection of the Coast Mountains, combined with warm winds from the Pacific Ocean, gives Vancouver a mild climate for its latitude. Average temperatures range from mid-30s Fahrenheit in winter to the mid-60s Fahrenheit in summer. Snow is common in the nearby mountains, but rare at sea level. Because Vancouver is so far north, there are less than 8 hours of darkness around the summer solstice. Although Vancouver is popularly believed to be a rainy city, measurable rainfall averages only 166 days out of the year.

Government

Vancouver has a mayor-city council form of government. The mayor and 10-members city council are elected to 2-year terms. Property taxes fund most city services, but the federal and provincial governments contribute funds toward improvements to the city's infrastructure.

Demographics

Roughly half of Vancouver's population is native-born, most of whom are descended from the British. Asian and western European immigrants are among the city's largest ethnic groups. The city's population is estimated at 545,000, and that of the entire metropolitan area is estimated at 2.2 million.

Economy

Vancouver's port drives most of Vancouver's economy. International freight shipping accounts for 75 million short tons annually. Vancouver is also a major port-of-call for cruise ships. Other industries include wholesale and retail trades, food processing, and lumber, and wood products. Vancouver is the largest financial center in western Canada, and nearly every large business in the province is headquartered here. Tourism is a rapidly growing industry, and the film and television industry is on the rise due to lower production costs in the country.

The History

The Vancouver area was inhabited by Salish Indians more than 2,000 years ago. The first European to visit the area was Spanish explorer Don Jose Marie Narvaez, in 1791. One year later, Captain George Vancouver of Britain sailed into what eventually became Burrard Inlet. The actual settlement was founded in 1865, when the Hastings Mill sawmill was built on the site. In 1884, the Canadian Pacific Railway chose the area for its western terminal. The city was incorporated in 1886. A major fire that same year destroyed much of the city, but reconstruction was swift.

Vancouver became the fastest-growing Canadian city between 1900 and 1910; the population swelled with immigrants from around the world, most of whom arrived to work in the fish- and wood-processing industries. The city grew further still during the Great Depression of the 1930s, as many unemployed Canadians tried (unsuccessfully) to find work. Vancouver began to prosper again during World War II, when it was the headquarters for the Canadian Army's coastal defense staff. Many skyscrapers and high-rise residential buildings were built following the war, forever changing the city's landscape.

The Sights and Sounds

Vancouver has a variety of museums and attractions to suit every taste. For art lovers, there is the Vancouver Museum, which frequently stages exhibitions from Canada and around the world. Its permanent collection provides a glimpse into the city's rich cultural heritage. The Vancouver Art Gallery is downtown and displays international art and artifacts both ancient and modern. The Vancouver

Maritime Museum in Heritage Harbour displays many historic seagoing vessels including the schooner St. Roch.

Scientific history is well represented in Vancouver's many science museums. Science World of British Columbia enables visitors to enjoy interactive exhibits while they learn about fascinating scientific discoveries of the past. At the H.R. MacMillan Space Centre, patrons can take part in a space-travel simulator and view multimedia shows and demonstrations at the museum's planetarium. The Vancouver Aquarium's extensive animal collection includes beluga whales, sea lions, dolphins, seals, and fascinating tropical fish. Special presentations include the popular shark dives and dolphin shows. To get a dramatic 360-degree view of the city and surrounding Coast Mountains, visit the Vancouver Lookout at Harbour Centre.

Vancouver also has beautiful and captivating outdoor treasures for nature lovers. The VanDusen Botanical Garden displays live plant collections, including species such as cherry trees, water lilies, and perennials. Leaf-peepers must visit in fall, when the trees display their full palette of colors. The Classical Chinese Garden is in the downtown area, and is named for Dr. Sun Yat Sen, the Father of Modern China. This authentic Chinese garden is an urban oasis of peace and tranquility. Guided tours are available, and a stop at the garden gift shop is a pleasant way to end your visit.

The Trivia

Fact: John Deighton, a former British sailor, founded the first saloon in Vancouver in 1865 to serve the loggers. He was known as Gassy Jack because of his talkativeness, and for a while Vancouver was known as Gas Town.

Fact: Vancouver's harbor is open all year because the harbor's water never freezes.

Fact: Vancouver's Chinatown is one the largest Chinese communities in North America. More than 17,000 people of Chinese descent live in the area, which is filled with restaurants, gift shops and nightclubs.

Why Vancouver Is a *50 plus one* City

Vancouver is a great city in the making. Like many locations in North America, it has a relatively short history and its potential lies in its future. The city dominates the Pacific coast of Canada, in the midst of natural beauty and a temperate climate. Vancouver is a fine place to visit any time of year.

48

Venice, Italy

The Basic Facts

Venice is one of the world's most famous and unusual cities. Venice developed as an independent city-state ruled by nobles and was briefly a colonial power in the 15th century.

Geography

Venice lies at 45 degrees 25 minutes north latitude and 12 degrees 18 minutes east longitude. The city's geography is unique among world cities; it is located on several islands in the Adriatic Sea northeast of Italy. The islands make up the historic center of Venice, but the mainland communities of Marghera and Mestre are also part of the city. The waterway that separates Venice from the mainland is the Venetian Lagoon, and a roadway connects the islands to the mainland. Venice is divided into six zones: San Marco, San Polo, Cannaregio, Dorsoduro, Castello and Santa Croce.

Climate

The weather in Venice can change drastically through the seasons; this is due in large part to the influence of Alpine and North African winds that blow across the area. Average temperatures range from the 80s Fahrenheit in summer–often spiking into the high 90s–and the lower 40s Fahrenheit in winter. Venice has high humidity regardless of the season.

Government

Venice is the center of an Italian government unit known as a comune. The chief executive of the comune is the mayor, who may delegate functions to subordinate councilors. Most officials are democratically elected.

Demographics

The population of the city of Venice is approximately 270,000 and the metropolitan area, which includes the city of Padua has a population of 1.6 million. More than 95 percent of the population is Italian; the remainder includes immigrants from Turkey, Ukraine, Tunisia and the Balkans

Since 1950 residents have moved from the islands to the Marghera and Mestre to escape Venice's annual floods. These areas also have better employment opportunities, a lower cost of living, and better housing than the city itself. New housing construction is essentially nonexistent on the islands of Venice because of geographic restrictions.

Economy

Tourism is the prime mover of Venice's economy since there are no manufacturing industries on the islands. Marghera and Mestre are the comune's industrial centers.

The History

In the 5th century Italians fled from invading Barbarians and poured into Venice. The early Venetian economy was based on fishing and trading, and by the 9th century was a major trading partner with the Italian mainland, Constantinople, and Africa. Venice was ruled by nobles and was a virtual city-state during this period of growth. Venice rivaled Genoa for trading privileges and the two regions battled in the 14th century; Venice eventually prevailed in 1380. The city's wealth and naval power helped to control the expansion of Islam into southern Europe.

In the 15th century Venice began to colonize the Mediterranean, and added Crete, Cyprus and Dalmatian (now part of Croatia) to its burgeoning empire. Venice also became a major trading center between Asia and the rest of Europe during this era. Trade declined in Venice after the discovery of America, as European trade shifted to the Atlantic coast. The Venetian empire was split between France and Austria when Napoleon occupied the city in the late 18th century.

Venice became part of the independent kingdom of Italy in 1866, and Marghera and Mestre began to industrialize in the early 20th century. After the Nazis seized Venice during World War II, the Allies bombed the mainland communities but spared the islands. Venice was devastated by a flood in 1966, during which many of the city's famous artworks were destroyed. The international community helped to restore the priceless artwork, and in the wake of the flood the city government instituted flood control measures to circumvent future disasters.

The Sights and Sounds

Unfortunately, years of environmental degradation and neglect have eroded much of Venice's storied history. Still, its romance and charm continue to attract tourists from around the world.

St. Mark's Basilica and the Plaza of St. Mark are perhaps the most famous of Venice's historical treasures. The Basilica was built to house the remains of St. Mark, who is the patron saint of Venice. This church is actually the third built on the site; the first was built in the 9th century. The Basilica's exterior is a fine example of Byzantine architecture, and its interior combines both Byzantine and Gothic elements. It is a grand and ornate Catholic church, and one of the world's great tourist attractions. Venice appropriated much of the church's art, mosaics and other riches from other areas of the Mediterranean; the renowned Triumphal Quadriga, a grouping of four bronze horses, were taken from Constantinople when that city was sacked during the Fourth Crusade.

Many consider St. Mark's Square to be loveliest in the world. On a typical day, visitors crowd the square to enjoy its elegant shops and cafes. The square is recognized worldwide for its ever-present flocks of pigeons. Napoleon is said to have remarked that the square is the finest drawing room in Europe.

The Campanile di San Marco, a 325-foot-tall bell tower, stood majestically in St. Mark's Square for 1,000 years—until it collapsed in 1902 for no apparent reason. It was rebuilt soon afterward in its original 16th century style. The view from the top of the tower is said to be the best in all of Venice.

The Doge's Palace, constructed of marble and limestone and finished in 1424, was the residence of the Doge (Duke), the seat of government, and the hall of justice. The prisoner's holding area is attached to the building by the famous Bridge of Sighs.

The Grand Canal is a two-mile main route through town. During the short voyage, sightseers pass some 200 Gothic and Renaissance palaces and grand estates that represent 1,000 years of history and culture. Locals suggest that visitors take a trip on the water bus once during the day and then again at night. Along the way are such sights as Ca' d'Oro (Golden House), which was built in the 15th century, its marble façade once enhanced with real gold; Ca' Rezzonico, a sumptuous palace built in the 1660s; and the Rialto Bridge, which dates from 1591 as the first stone bridge across the canal.

The Church of Saints John and Paul, second only to St. Mark's in size and opulence, was the traditional site where Doges were crowned. It was built in the

13th and 14th centuries and is the resting place of some 25 Doges.

The Trivia

Fact: After Venice defeated Genoa in 1380, the city celebrated the victory with a symbolic marriage ceremony, in which the Doges were wed with the Adriatic Sea. The ceremony was celebrated with great pomp on a huge gilded gondola called the Bucentaur.

Fact: Venice was essential to the Fourth Crusade which lasted from 1201 to 1204. Venice provided the transportation necessary for the crusaders and joined them in battle against the Byzantine Empire. The 4th Crusade ended with the invasion and defeat of Constantinople.

Fact: Venice's 150 canals take the place of streets. Boats rather than cars are the city's primary means of transportation. The famous flat-bottomed gondolas were employed for centuries but have been replaced by motorboats and waterbuses. More than 400 bridges traverse the canals, and narrow alleys called calli run between the buildings and the islands.

Fact: Until the mid-1970's, Venice sank at a rate of about one-fifth an inch per year. Experts believed that well drilling was largely responsible for this phenomenon. Although the Italian government later restricted the drilling process, many believe that the city is still sinking today.

Why Venice Is a *50 plus one* City

Venice is a romantic, artistic, historically significant, and unique city. Tourists often outnumber residents in this city that has attracted sightseers for hundreds of years.

Vienna, Austria

The Basic Facts

Vienna is the capital of Austria and the country's largest city. It is a leading cultural, political and economic center, and one of Europe's most beautiful and culturally rich cities.

Geography

Vienna lies at 48 degrees 13 minutes north latitude and 16 degrees 22 minutes east longitude. The city is located in northeastern Austria on the south bank of the Danube River, in a narrow plain between the Carpathian Mountains and the Alps. Just east of Vienna is a mountain gap through the Carpathians that helped the city become a major trading center.

Climate

Vienna has a climate that is typically dry and largely influenced by the rest of continental Europe. Frigid winds from Eastern Europe and Russia can bring cold winters. Average temperatures range from the 30s Fahrenheit in winter to the upper 70s Fahrenheit in summer.

Government

Vienna is the capital of the Republic of Austria and is both a city and a federal province. The city's mayor is also the governor of the province, and the city council also acts as the provincial government. Both the mayor and city council are democratically elected.

Demographics

Austrians constitute the majority of Vienna residents; the city also has a large number of Czechs and Hungarians. German is the primary language of Vienna. The city's population is 1.6 million and the metropolitan area's population is roughly 2.2 million.

Economy

Vienna is the center of the nation's industrial economy. Manufacturing industries include chemicals, clothing, leather goods and medicine. Tourism and government services are also important to the local economy.

The History

The area of present-day Vienna was originally a Celtic settlement founded around 500 B.C. In the 1st century A.D. the Roman Empire used Vindobona (the empire's name for Vienna) as a base to guard against invading Germanic forces. The Emperor Marcus Aurelius lived there until his death in 180. The Goths sacked Vindobona in the 4th century and ousted the Romans. A series of invaders occupied the area until the 12th century, when Leopold I of Austria assumed control.

In the 13th century Henry II of Austria moved the capital to Vienna, and in 1281 the city became the official residence of the House of Habsburg. In 1857 the walls of the original city were razed to permit expansion; the walls' original location became the tree-lined boulevard known as the Ring. The city survived sieges by the Turks and their Hungarian allies over the next several centuries, and by the 18th century began a new set of fortifications. The city also began to erect some magnificent buildings during this period.

In the late 19th and early 20th centuries, Vienna flourished as a center of the arts and sciences, and in 1918 became the capital of the First Austrian Republic. During this period, Vienna improved its urban infrastructure and built new housing for the city's poor.

Austria was annexed to Germany in the Anschluss of 1938, and in March of that year Hitler's troops entered Vienna and were greeted warmly by crowds. Allied bombing during World War II heavily damaged Vienna, and the Nazi extermination of Austrian Jews decimated the city's population. At the Potsdam Conference in 1945, Austria and Vienna were each divided into four occupation zones. Austria was reunited as a neutral state in 1955 and Vienna again became the nation's capital.

The Sights and Sounds

The old-world culture, art and architecture of Vienna make it a comfortable and charming city. It is also an accessible city; most of the major sights are in the oldest section of the city within the Ring.

Vienna is well regarded for its museums, which are some of the finest in Europe.

The Albertina is popular for its collection of drawings, sketches, engravings, and etchings by the Old Masters. Efforts have been made in recent years to restore the Albertina and to enhance the quality of its exhibits. Classical music fans will enjoy the Mozart Memorial Rooms, a small museum in a house near St. Stephen's Cathedral. Mozart lived here for about 4 years, and today a full array of Mozart memorabilia is on display. From this intimate apartment, progress to the House of Music devoted to the classical greats, including Haydn, Strauss, Beethoven and Mahler. Individual rooms are dedicated to each composer and many display the artists' original scores.

Conflict, war, and ethnic chaos occurred throughout Austria's history and the history of its predecessor, the Austro-Hungarian Empire. The Museum of Military History displays the full range of arms and armaments implemented in the region's major conflicts. A notable exhibit contains the car in which Archduke Franz Ferdinand was assassinated; his death led to the start of World War I.

In 2001 the Imperial Court Stables became the Museum Quarter, a vast cultural center that includes four museums, a concert hall, theatres, dance facilities, exhibition halls, and even a children's museum. The museum is conveniently located near the Hofburg Imperial Palace.

Much of the Hofburg dates to the 13th century. This glamorous, formal complex of buildings and courtyards currently serves as the residence of the Austrian president.

On Sundays and religious holidays, the world-famous Vienna Boys Choir performs at the court chapel in the Hofburg. Their High Mass performances are so popular that tickets are expensive and in short supply. The court chapel is a small venue, but lucky ticket holders will cherish the experience.

The revered Vienna Philharmonic Orchestra performs in the fabulous Musikverein, a beautiful concert hall where the orchestra performs its annual New Year's Concert. The Staatsoper is the home of the popular Vienna State Opera. Much of the original structure was destroyed during World War II, but in 1955 the restored building opened to great acclaim.

Near the Hofburg is another must-see: the Spanish Riding School, the training grounds of the renowned Lipizzan horses. Formal shows take place on Saturday and Sunday in the indoor Winter Riding School, where the beauty and grace of these majestic creatures are enhanced by the hall's pure white walls and crystal chandeliers. If weekend shows sell out–which they often do–tickets to morning practice sessions during the week are also available.

The cathedral known as Stephansdom is an architectural masterpiece, its Gothic spires reaching heavenward to dominate the city's landscape. The church is a literal maze of tombs, altars, and sculptures. Also heavily damaged during World War II, the church has not lost its medieval mystery and fascination. Many Habsburg royals are entombed in the underground crypt. Those visitors able to manage the 343 steps up the south tower will be rewarded with a delightful view of Vienna.

Outside of the inner zone, the Schönbrunn Palace is popularly known as the Versailles of Vienna, which exemplifies Baroque art and architecture at its best. The palace and formal gardens were built by the Habsburgs between 1696 and 1713. Guided tours are available, although only a fraction of this sprawling complex is open to the public. State dinners and other formal events are held here.

Vienna is known for its numerous restaurants, cafes and coffee houses, and especially its famous torts and pastries. Evening in Vienna offers a wealth of opportunities as well, from theatres and concerts to nightclubs and wine taverns. There truly is something for everyone in this world-famous city.

The Trivia

Fact: Vienna attracted noteworthy composers such as Brahms, Mahler, Strauss and Schoenberg during its golden age of the late 19th and early 20th centuries. Also at this time, the important Austrian neurologist Sigmund Freud developed his theories and techniques in psychoanalysis.

Fact: Vienna is the home of international organizations such as the International Atomic Energy Agency and the Organization of Petroleum Exporting Countries (OPEC).

Fact: In 1961 the city hosted the historic Vienna Summit, at which U.S. President John F. Kennedy and Soviet Premier Nikita Khrushchev attempted to resolve a variety of diplomatic concerns. The conference ultimately proved to be a failure, however, as the Cuban Missile Crisis of 1962 plunged the world further into the lengthy Cold War.

Why Vienna Is a *50 plus one* City

Vienna has constantly survived wars and other conflicts to retain its greatness, sophistication, and old-world culture. The entire city is a treasure to be seen and cherished.

Washington, D.C., United States

The Basic Facts

Washington, D.C. (also known as Washington or D.C.), is the capital of the United States and is one of the nation's most beautiful and historic cities. Apart from its status as the seat of the federal government, it has a wealth of historical monuments and museums.

Geography

Washington lies at 38 degrees 50 minutes north latitude and 77 degrees west longitude. It is located along the Potomac River and is bordered by Maryland and Virginia. The city itself is composed of four quadrants arranged in grids, and its metropolitan area consists of the District of Columbia and 26 counties in West Virginia, Virginia and Maryland.

Climate

Washington's weather varies significantly throughout the year. Summers are usually hot and humid, especially in the city center. Winters are often cold and snowy, and heavy snowfalls are common. Annual temperatures vary widely, from the mid-20s Fahrenheit in winter to the low 90s Fahrenheit in summer.

Government

Washington's local government is unique among U.S. cities. Although the city's mayor and council are democratically elected, the federal government has power to veto any legislation passed by the council. In the 1870s, Congress took over government rule of Washington after it found that the city's governor mismanaged funds. Because the city is a government entity and not a state, it has no representation in the U.S. Congress—a fact that has led to much consternation among Washingtonians, who believe that they deserve equal status in the federal government.

Demographics

Washington's population of 550,000 is small in comparison to most major world cities, but the metropolitan area's population is currently 4.8 million and ever on the increase.

Economy

Washington's economy is dominated by the federal government and non-governmental organizations including think tanks and lobbyists. The service industry is accordingly large to accommodate this significant workforce. Tourism is vital to the economy as well; millions arrive every year to visit the city's many historical sites. Trade and industry are virtually nonexistent.

The History

The French-born architect Charles L'Enfant designed the street plan for the city, and chose the Capitol Building as its focal point. The U.S. Congress held its first session at the Capitol in 1800.

British soldiers invaded Washington in 1814 during the War of 1812 and most public buildings were destroyed by fire but by 1819 the buildings were restored. A territorial government was established in Washington after the Civil War, and the city began to improve its infrastructure. After World War II, Washington's population declined in the 1950s as many residents moved to the expanding suburbs in the metropolitan area.

Washingtonians began demanding more control over their government, and in 1967 President Lyndon Johnson reorganized the city government to include a mayor and city council.

The Sights and Sounds

Tourists flock to Washington because there is so much to see and do in a relatively small area. The city has a useful public transportation system, and many of the city's districts are easily accessible on foot.

The National Mall is the heart and soul of Washington. Locals and visitors alike fill the place each day to enjoy life, view the sights, and gather for recreation or political purposes. It is a vast open space roughly two miles long, bounded by the U.S. Capitol and the Lincoln Memorial at either end and the Washington Monument at its center. The Mall's hundreds of cherry trees—a gift from Japan in 1912—are abloom each spring.

Washington D.C. is well known for its memorials to past presidents. The

Washington Monument, completed in 1884, is a marble, granite, and sandstone obelisk that rises 555 feet over the National Mall. This monument, named for the country's first president, is beautifully mirrored in the adjacent Reflecting Pool. The Lincoln Memorial is a masterpiece of U.S. architecture, and undoubtedly the single most evocative structure in the nation. Built as a tribute to the nation's 16th president, Abraham Lincoln, its marble-and-limestone architecture recalls the Doric temples of Greece. Within its large open-air interior, a 19-foot-tall of the seated president gazes somberly out onto the Mall. The Jefferson Memorial is visible from the Mall, located in West Potomac Park on the Tidal Basin. The city's beloved cherry trees grow and bloom here. A 19-foot-tall bronze statue of Thomas Jefferson, the architect of the Declaration of Independence, stands majestically under the memorial's rotunda. The Franklin Delano Roosevelt Memorial, completed in 1997, is a new arrival on the Mall. Four outdoor galleries—one for each term of Roosevelt's presidency—are enhanced by a series of waterfalls and pools.

Among the many memorials to fallen war heroes on the National Mall, three cannot be overlooked. The National World War II Memorial is a more elaborate display, with 56 pillars surrounding a central plaza. The Korean War Veterans Memorial, dedicated in 1995, is a triangular arrangement with life-sized statues of soldiers on patrol. Its design provokes contemplation of the horrors of war and the terrible hardships that the soldiers endured. The Vietnam Veterans Memorial Wall, an expansive yet unobtrusive monument of black granite, is inscribed with the names of the more than 58,000 dead or missing who served in the Vietnam War. Families, friends, and others are drawn to the memorial to pay their respects to the men and women who gave their lives for their country. Reverent visitors fall silent to witness loved ones touching the names of those they knew.

A grassy ellipse connects the National Mall to the White House, surely one of the most frequently photographed and recognized residences of the world. Recently-enhanced security has unfortunately limited tours of the building's interior, but its exterior is breathtaking in its design. Among its 132 rooms are the Oval Office, Lincoln's bedroom, and the Blue Room, where heads of state are traditional received.

The Smithsonian Institution is a complex of 19 museums, each dedicated to a distinct period of art or science history. Of note are the National Air and Space Museum, with the world's largest collection of aircraft and spacecraft, the National Museum of American History, the National Museum of Natural History, and the Freer Gallery of Art.

The Capitol Hill area is a must for first-time visitors. The U.S. Capitol building, the Supreme Court Building, and the Library of Congress are all located within a short distance of one another, yet security restrictions periodically restrict access to these areas.

The Georgetown neighborhood of Washington is an enclave for the rich and the powerful. Charming old homes, cafes, restaurants and bars line its streets. Georgetown University, the oldest Jesuit university in the United States, is located here.

The Trivia

Fact: On September 11, 2001, terrorists hijacked a commercial airliner and crashed it into the Pentagon, the headquarters of the U.S. Department of Defense. Although all passengers and crew perished in the crash, there were few fatalities on the ground because that area of the building was unoccupied due to construction.

Fact: In 1862, slavery was abolished in Washington D.C. before President Lincoln signed the Emancipation Proclamation, which would abolish the practice nationwide. Slave owners who swore an oath of loyalty to the United States exchanged their slaves for an average of $300 each.

Fact: The steps of the Lincoln Memorial have served as a fitting backdrop to many speeches, including the famous I Have a Dream speech delivered by Martin Luther King, Jr. in 1963. The footage of the speech figures prominently in documentaries of the city's history.

Fact: Ford's Theatre, where Abraham Lincoln was assassinated in 1865, is both a museum containing Lincoln memorabilia and a venue for live performances.

Fact: All 50 U.S. states are represented in the names of the city's diagonal roads.

Why Washington, D.C. Is a *50 plus one* City

As the center of United States government, as a planned city with world-famous monuments, as the repository of the nation's treasures, and as a city famous for its restaurants, people and power brokers, it is fabulous!

Smart, Friendly and Informative

The *50 plus one* series are thorough and detailed guides covering a wide range of topics–both personal and business related, supplying you, the reader, the information and resources you need and want in an easy-to-read format.

**50 plus one Tips
When Remodeling Your Home**
by William Resch

**50 plus one Greatest
Sports Heroes of All Times
(North American Edition)**
by Paul J. Christopher

**50 plus one Tips to
Building a Retirement Nest Egg**
by Linda M. Magoon and Poonum Vasishth

**50 plus one Ways to
Improve Your Study Habits**
by Stephen Edwards

**50 plus one Tips When
Hiring & Firing Employees**
Edited by Linda M. Magoon & Donna de St. Aubin

**50 plus one Questions
When Buying a Car**
by Stephen Edwards

**50 plus one Tips to
Preventing Identity Theft**
by Elizabeth Drake

**50 plus one Great Books
You Should Have Read
(and probably didn't)**
by George Walsh

**50 plus one
Questions to Ask Your Doctor**
by Elizabeth Drake

Titles from Encouragement Press

Available from bookstores everywhere or directly from Encouragement Press. Bulk discounts are available, for information please call 1.253.303.0033

50 plus one Series			
Title	Price	Qty.	Subtotal
Greatest Cities in the World You Should Visit	$14.95 U.S./$19.95 Can.		
Tips When Remodeling Your Home	$14.95 U.S./$19.95 Can.		
Greatest Sports Heroes of All Times (North American Edition)	$14.95 U.S./$19.95 Can.		
Tips to Building A Retirement Nest Egg	$14.95 U.S./$19.95 Can.		
Ways To Improve Your Study Habits	$14.95 U.S./$19.95 Can.		
Tips When Hiring & Firing Employees	$14.95 U.S./$19.95 Can.		
Questions When Buying a Car	$14.95 U.S./$19.95 Can.		
Tips to Preventing Identity Theft	$14.95 U.S./$19.95 Can.		
Great Books You Should Have Read (and probably didn't)	$14.95 U.S./$19.95 Can.		
Questions to Ask Your Doctor	$14.95 U.S./$19.95 Can.		

Subtotal	
IL residents add 8.75% sales tax	
Shipping & Handling*	
Total	

* Shipping & Handling

U.S. Orders:	Canadian Orders:
$3.35 for first book	$7.00 for first book
$2.00 for ea. add'l book	$5.00 for ea. add'l book

4 Ways to Order

Phone: 1.773.262.6565

Web: *www.encouragementpress.com*

Fax: 1.773.262.9765

Mail: Encouragement Press LLC
       1261 W. Glenlake
       Chicago, IL 60660

Please make checks payable to:
Encouragement Press, LLC
*(Orders must be prepaid. We regret that
we are unable to ship orders without
payment or purchase order)*

Payment Method (check one)
❏ **Check enclosed** ❏ **Visa** ❏ **MasterCard**

_____

card number

_____

signature

_____

Name as it appears on card

expiration date _____

P.O. #_____

Encouragement Press, LLC
1261 W. Glenlake • Chicago, IL 60660 • *sales@encouragementpress.com*